CW01499187

THE FIRST ENGLISH CONQUEST OF CANADA: WITH SOME ACCOUNT OF THE EARLIEST SETTLEMENTS IN NOVA SCOTIA AND NEWFOUNDLAND

Published @ 2017 Trieste Publishing Pty Ltd

ISBN 9780649583454

The First English Conquest of Canada: With Some Account of the Earliest Settlements in Nova Scotia and Newfoundland by Henry Kirke

Except for use in any review, the reproduction or utilisation of this work in whole or in part in any form by any electronic, mechanical or other means, now known or hereafter invented, including xerography, photocopying and recording, or in any information storage or retrieval system, is forbidden without the permission of the publisher, Trieste Publishing Pty Ltd, PO Box 1576 Collingwood, Victoria 3066 Australia.

All rights reserved.

Edited by Trieste Publishing Pty Ltd.
Cover @ 2017

This book is sold subject to the condition that it shall not, by way of trade or otherwise, be lent, re-sold, hired out, or otherwise circulated without the publisher's prior consent in any form or binding or cover other than that in which it is published and without a similar condition including this condition being imposed on the subsequent purchaser.

www.triestepublishing.com

HENRY KIRKE

THE FIRST ENGLISH CONQUEST OF CANADA: WITH SOME ACCOUNT OF THE EARLIEST SETTLEMENTS IN NOVA SCOTIA AND NEWFOUNDLAND

Trieste

THE

FIRST ENGLISH

CONQUEST OF CANADA;

WITH SOME ACCOUNT OF

The Earliest Settlements in Nova Scotia and Newfoundland.

BY

HENRY KIRKE, M.A., B.C.L., Oxon.,

AUTHOR OF "THURSTAN MEVERELL," &c., &c.

———◆———

LONDON:

BEMROSE & SONS, 21, PATERNOSTER ROW; AND DERBY.

1871.

226. i. 239.

TO

ADMIRAL

SIR HENRY PRESCOTT, G.C.B.,

AT ONE TIME

GOVERNOR OF NEWFOUNDLAND,

THIS BOOK

IS

WITH AFFECTION AND RESPECT,

DEDICATED,

BY

THE AUTHOR.

PREFACE.

THE opening of the Record Office to the public has made us acquainted with such a vast amount of material, never before accessible to readers, which serves to illustrate the History of England, that it may be taken for granted that the whole of that History will have to be re-written by the light of the new facts which are submitted to us. So great are the changes resulting from such a wholesale discovery of documents, that our belief in the main facts of English History, such as we were taught in our childhood, is in danger of being entirely subverted; and when we leave the beaten track, and attempt, like Macaulay and Froude, to analyse the actions and motives of our leading History makers, we are overwhelmed by the mass of documentary evidence which is now offered to us.

If, therefore, we are to profit by the Records so lately exhumed from obscurity, the received histories of our national story must be overhauled, their doubtful facts and dates rectified, their ambiguities explained, and their numerous *lacunæ* filled up.

The following little book is an attempt to perform these duties to one page of English History; a page somewhat neglected, not dogeared from excessive reading, but almost unknown, not so much from its want of value or its dulness, but rather on account of the many blanks which gape in its narrative, so as to reduce it almost to vacuity. The subject may be considered Colonial rather than English, but at this time (the 17th Century) the Colonies as such could barely be called existing. Patents were issued by different European sovereigns to their subjects, granting unlimited rights over territories unbounded, except by the imagination of the grantors; for which patents considerable sums were exacted, and careful provision was made to protect the rights of the Crown in case of success; but the government of any country rarely, if ever, supported the adventurers who left their shores, though they often, as we shall see, deprived them of the fruits of their exertions. The whole Colonial

History of this period is a continual struggle between the different European nations for the possession of America; and though it has been thought convenient for the purpose of reference to arrange together all the papers relating to the countries which eventually became British Colonies, it is not to be supposed that they were considered to be Colonial when they were written, or were separated from the Foreign correspondence of the period. Mr. Sainsbury is in error when he states in the Preface to his "Calendar of State Papers, Colonial Series, 1574–1660," "The Papers in the State Paper Office are arranged upon principles which are extremely simple. Derived from the offices of the Secretaries of State, they fall almost as of course, into three great branches or divisions, corresponding with the offices whence they are transmitted. Those for the office of the Home Secretary constitute one principal division or series of volumes, technically termed the Domestic, with a subdivision for Ireland; the papers for the office of the Foreign Secretary form a second or Foreign division or series; whilst those for the Colonial office are arranged in a third division or series, named the Colonial. The present volume is a

Calendar of the last named series of papers only
from the year 1574, the date of the earliest paper
down to the year 1660," whereas from 1574 to
1660, there were only two Secretaries of State, who
transacted the business of the Home and Foreign
offices indiscriminately, or made such arrangements
as suited their own convenience. A little further
on, Mr. Sainsbury confesses that "During this early
period a separation of the Colonial from the Domestic
or other series, and a classification of the former
upon the principles adopted in the correspondence
of a later date, has been found to be extremely
difficult." At the same time I must record my deep
obligations to Mr. Sainsbury's admirable Calendar;
without his assistance, the discovery of the necessary
papers would have been indeed wearisome, if not
impossible.

The papers in the Record Office relating to Canada,
Acadia or Nova Scotia, and Newfoundland, are numerous and continuous from the year 1621 to 1660,
with the exception of the period from 1640 to 1649,
during which years we find no papers relating to
any of these countries. This was owing to the
Civil War in England, which engrossed the attention of all public men, and prevented them from

taking any notice of the different settlements in America. I have carefully studied all the papers which seemed likely to throw any light upon the subject of this work, in which labour I have been materially assisted by Byam Martin Prescott, Esq., to whom I offer my sincere thanks.

H. K.

THE FIRST ENGLISH CONQUEST OF CANADA.

INTRODUCTORY CHAPTER.

CHARLES I. succeeded to the throne on the 27th of March, 1625, in the twenty-fifth year of his age. James had bequeathed to his successor an exhausted treasury, and personal debts amounting to seven hundred thousand pounds; and the accession and marriage of the new King entailed upon him great but necessary expenses. However, he met his new Parliament with cheerfulness; and, exposing the state of his finances, threw himself upon their bounty, and requested a liberal subsidy. He could not be held responsible for the extravagance of his father, and the

B

money required was only to carry out the
vote of the last Parliament.   But there were
many circumstances to damp his expectations;
in the Upper House many of the Peers
looked with an evil eye upon the ascendancy
of Buckingham, and were anxious to oppose
the Government in hopes of discomfiting
the favourite.   At the head of this party was
the Earl of Pembroke, a nobleman of high
position and influence in the House.   In the
Commons, the Puritans had formed themselves
into a body determined to oppose the spread
of what they considered Popish tendencies;
the dread of Popery haunted them like an
evil dream; they saw it in the gaieties of
the court, in the ceremonies of the church,
and the distinctions of the hierarchy.   The
King's marriage was an offence to them; he
had promised not to marry one Papist, and
now he was going to marry another.   The
union of these two parties, the one opposed
to Buckingham and the other opposed to
Popery, gave great strength to the opposition,

and enlisted the sympathies of the people, who considered that they were fighting the battle of civil and religious liberty against the advocates of slavery and superstition.

The first two years of his reign was spent by Charles in continual struggles with his Parliament. They would grant him no money, and when he pressed for a subsidy, they presented a petition of grievances, and said they would grant the money when their petition was answered. The Earl of Bristol accused Buckingham before the House of Lords of various crimes and misdemeanours, and the House of Commons had impeached him before the Lords; and so strong was their language against him, that Sir John Eliot compared him, for lust, ambition, and rapacity, to Sejanus, the profligate minister of Tiberius Cæsar. Charles, determined to shield his favourite, dissolved Parliament in a transport of fury.

Reduced now to the greatest extremity for want of money, Charles proceeded to the

most extreme measures. He determined to
raise a forced loan from all noblemen, gentlemen, and merchants of estate; and for that
purpose sent inquisitors through all the
counties in England, to extract a sum of
money from each in proportion to the amount
which he had paid at the last general
subsidy. In addition to these arbitrary
measures, the public heard with grief that
the allies of England, under the King of
Denmark, had suffered a great defeat at the
hands of Count Tilley, at Luttern; that the
whole of Lower Saxony was abandoned to
Ferdinand, and the cause of Protestantism in
Germany was itself at stake. The King's
affairs were in such a critical state that the
only course which seemed to offer any prospect, was to make peace with Spain, and to
be reconciled to his Parliament. Instead of
which, he proceeded to involve himself in a
war with the King of France, whose sister
he had married, and whose alliance he had
always courted.

As the conquest of Canada and Acadia by the English was the only result of this insane war, it will be better, before we turn to consider that conquest in detail, to give a short account of the causes which provoked the war, the operations carried out in Europe, and the ignoble peace which brought it to a termination.

When the Duke of Buckingham had visited Paris two years previously to conduct Henrietta Maria into England, he had dazzled the French capital by the splendour of his dress and retinue. During his residence there he had received much attention from the French ladies, but he presumed to fix his affections upon the young and beautiful Queen Anne of Austria, and to address her in terms of passionate adoration. Watched and warned by the servants of Richelieu, he was kept within the bounds of decorum, but he parted with the Queen in tears; and upon his journey home he left the Princess with her attendants at Boulogne, hastened back to Paris, obtained

admittance to the Queen's bed-chamber, and,
throwing himself on his knees before her,
avowed his passion. The Queen, alarmed
and astounded, ordered him to leave her;
but the Duke only returned home more
infatuated, and nursing his mad passion. To
forward his schemes, he obtained from Charles
the appointment of Ambassador to Paris, but
Richelieu refused to receive him. Louis XIII.
had naturally a strong repugnance to him,
and no artifice could induce him or his minister
to receive the impetuous Duke at Paris. This
slight so enraged Buckingham that he determined to be revenged, and formed one of
the principal reasons why he urged upon
Charles the declaration of war against France.
Charles was himself very indignant with the
French King. At the time of his marriage
it had been agreed that Louis should assist
the Protestant States in their war with
Ferdinand; but this treaty had never been
signed, and now the French King repudiated
it altogether. The Protestants of France were

at this time in rebellion, and Charles hoped that he might restore his waning popularity in England by some vigorous action on their behalf; so, in this frame of mind, he lent a willing ear to the emissary of the discontented party in France, and agreed to send an army to La Rochelle to co-operate with the Duke of Rohan and the French Protestants. During the war with Spain, letters of marque had been issued to English ships, and vessels belonging to all nations had been swept into British ports, under the pretence of carrying Spanish goods. This occasioned great irritation amongst the nations aggrieved, and Louis not only intimated his displeasure, but in retaliation laid an embargo upon all English ships in French ports. Long and tedious recriminations on both sides followed, till at length both Kings signed a declaration of war.

A large armament was collected in the English ports, which was ostensibly to support the Palsgrave and chastise the Algerines; but the King of France was not deceived, and he immediately entered into an alliance, offensive and defensive with Spain, against the common enemy. At length Buckingham sailed, having under his command forty-two ships of war, and thirty-four transports, containing seven regiments of nine hundred men each, a squadron of cavalry, and a great number of French Protestants. A few days brought them to Rochelle, the head of the insurrection; but with so much secrecy had the expedition been planned that the Rochellois were ignorant of its designs, and refused to admit Buckingham and his troops within their walls. It is needless to pursue the history of this disastrous campaign; Buckingham wanted every qualification for a commander, except personal courage; Burroughs, his only efficient lieutenant, was killed at an early stage of the proceedings; one disastrous blunder was only succeeded by another; and at length the Duke with difficulty withdrew the remains of his discomfited armament, and returned to

England with the loss of more than two thousand men and twenty pairs of colours. This expedition excited the greatest dismay in the States, in the Prince Palatine, and the King of Denmark, who all urged upon Charles the suicidal character of his conduct, and offered their good services to bring about a reconciliation between him and the King of France. But it was of no avail. Smarting under his discomfiture, and the murmurs of the English people, Buckingham was collecting another armament to raise the siege of Rochelle. Ever since his last failure, the Rochellois had not ceased to importune King Charles for help, imploring him not to abandon them to their fate. On the other hand, Richelieu was making superhuman efforts to accomplish their destruction. Not only had he collected a vast army, which completely isolated the city on the one hand, but he was building a mole across the mouth of the harbour, to prevent all access from the sea. This stupendous work, despite several failures, was now progressing rapidly, and the unfortunate people of Rochelle saw their hope of succour becoming daily smaller and smaller. Their prayers moved the heart of the English King, and the Earl of Denbigh sailed from Plymouth with a numerous fleet; which arriving at Rochelle, did nothing, but after remaining for seven days off the entrance to the harbour, returned to England. Here the fleet was reinforced and revictualled, and placed under the command of Buckingham, who was preparing to sail when his career was stopped short by the knife of Felton. The expedition was not stopped by the death of Buckingham; the command was given to the Earl of Lindsey, who shortly arrived before Rochelle; but after manœuvering for five days in front of the harbour, and making two ineffectual attempts to enter, he returned to Spithead, and Rochelle immediately afterwards surrendered at discretion. Charles had now begun to repent the folly which had hurried him into war with both France and

Spain. He was so hampered by his quarrel with his Parliament, that he could do nothing against his enemies, and, indeed, was much indebted to them for their forbearance. Whether from generosity or contempt Philip of Spain returned him, without ransom, all the prisoners taken at Cadiz, and Louis all that were captured in the Island of Rhè. By the mediation of the Venetian Ambassador peace was proposed between England and France; few difficulties were made, and those were quickly overcome. Louis waived his right to the St. Esprit, a ship of war illegally captured by the English, and Charles surrendered the French Protestants to the clemency of their Sovereign. All conquests on both sides were to be restored, by which article Canada and Acadia, which had been captured by the English, were restored to the French Crown. Such were the results of this foolish war, begun by Charles and his favourite to satisfy an angry impulse; carried on with a weakness and incapacity which has scarcely ever been equalled, it was ended by a disgraceful and one-sided peace.

It is pleasant to turn from this spectacle of feeble mismanagement, to consider the only event which cast any lustre, during the war, upon the British arms, and which added, for a time, a vast territory to the British empire. The conquest of Canada and Acadia, and the defeat of the French fleet in North America, is the one bright spot in a disastrous campaign; but all the results of that enterprise were thrown away by the English King, who seemed strangely blind to the interests of the nation, and who wished to patch up a peace at any price, that he might prosecute without hindrance his struggle with the Parliament.

The conquest of Canada must always be regarded as a striking example of the private enterprise of British merchants. It was accomplished solely by the exertions and at the expense of some London merchants, who formed themselves into a Company of " Merchant Adventurers," as they were then called, for the purpose of establishing a lucrative trade with Canada, and the countries bordering upon the St. Lawrence. They fitted out ships, and obtained a patent from the King, giving them authority to found a plantation, and letters of marque to enable them to seize French and Spanish vessels and goods. The usual way of carrying on a naval war at this time was for the King to issue letters of marque to the captains of ships fitted out by private persons, giving them authority to seize and appropriate the goods and ships of the enemy. English ships were often fitted out by adventurers, or men of desperate fortunes, who hoped, by a lucky cruise, to fill their empty purses, and at the same time do good service to their country. In the unsettled state of maritime law which existed at this period, all merchant ships were more or less armed, and it took little preparation to fit one of them out as a man-of-war. The Royal Navy of England could hardly be said to exist at the beginning of the seventeenth century. At the time of the Spanish Armada, England could only muster thirteen small ships of war, and the majority of the vessels which went forth so boldly to meet the huge Spanish three-deckers, were merchant vessels which had been seized by the Government, and hastily and imperfectly armed, or which had been fitted out by the patriotism of their owners. In the year 1600 the naval forces of England amounted to thirty-six ships of war, all of small burden.[1]   There

1 The "Royal Sovereign," a ship of the first class, was built in 1637, and was considered a prodigy for size and strength. It is thus described in the "Angliæ Notitia," published in 1671 :—"The 'Royal Sovereign,' being a ship of the first rate and rank, built in the year 1637, is in length by the keel 127 feet, in breadth by the beam 47 feet, in depth 49 feet, her draught of water 21 feet ; of burden in all 2,072 tons ; and 1,554 tons besides guns, tackle, &c. This mighty moving castle hath 6 anchors, whereof the biggest weighs 6,000 lbs., and the least 4,300 lbs. It hath 14 cables, whereof the greatest is 21 inches in compass, and weighs 9,000 lbs., her least cable being 8 inches in compass, weighing nearly 1,300 lbs. To the 'Royal Sovereign' belong 18 masts and yards, whereof the greatest, called the main mast, is 175 feet long, her main yard 97 feet long, and her main top 15 feet diameter. She hath 10 different sorts of sails, of several names, whereof her greatest sail, called her main course (together with her bonnet), contains 1,640 yards of canvas, Ipswich double, and the least sail, called the fore top gallant sail, contains 130 yards of canvas. The charge for one complete set of sails for the 'Royal Sovereign' is

was one large ship of one thousand tons, and carrying thirty guns, the others were vessels of one hundred tons burden, and carrying seven or eight guns. The genius of Cromwell and Blake, and the naval wars with the Dutch, quickly brought about a change in our naval power, so that in 1670 England possessed more than one hundred and sixty men-of-war, carrying nearly five thousand guns. The whole naval force of England was foiled and discomfited before Rochelle, but a few merchant ships, armed and fitted out by a London company, achieved a great success over the French arms in America, chiefly through the genius and good fortune of Sir David Kirke, the leader of the English squadron.

£404 sterling money. The weight of the sea store, in point of ground tackle and other cordage, is 60 tons, 800 and odd lbs. She carries a long boat of 50 feet, a pinnace of 36 feet, and a skiff of 27 feet long. The weight of her rigging is 33 tons. She hath 3 tire of guns, all of brass, whereof there are 44 in her upper tire, 34 in her second tire, and 22 in her lower tire, in all 100 guns. She carries in all, of officers and soldiers and marines, 700 men. Finally, her whole charge for wages, victuals, ammunition, wear and tear, for every month at sea costs the King £3,500 sterling, as hath been computed by a very skilful person. The cost of building a ship of the first rate, together with guns, tackle, and rigging, doth ordinarily amount to £26,000."

CHAPTER I.

Birth and Parentage of Gervase Kirke—Bound Apprentice in London—State of England under Queen Elizabeth—English Merchant Adventurers—Expedition of Sir Francis Drake—Marriage of Gervase Kirke—Birth of David and Lewis Kirke—Formation of the Canada Company—Early History of Canada—Expedition of Cartier—Of De la Roche—Voyages of M. de Chauvin and M. de Monts—Expedition of Champlain—Formation of the Company of New France—The French Fleet Sails for Acadia.

ON the 30th of December, in the year of Grace 1566, Thurston Kirke, of Greenhill, in the parish of Norton, in the county of Derby, married Frances, daughter of Jerome[1] Blythe, Esq., of Norton Hall. The bridegroom was a cadet of the family of Kirke, of Chapel-en-

1 Jerome Blythe married Anne, daughter and co-heiress of Richard Eyre, of Offerton, co. Derby, Esq., and sister and co-heiress of Ralph Eyre, of Oxspring, co. York.

le-Frith, an Anglo-Danish race of freeholders
and inferior gentry in the county of Derby
for several hundred years before the date given
above. The bride belonged to an old family
of gentle blood, resident at Norton for many
generations. Though not distinguished above
their fellows in arms or politics, the family
of Blythe[1] could boast of two of its members,
brothers, and both bishops, viz., John Blythe,
Bishop of Salisbury, and Geoffrey Blythe,
Bishop of Lichfield and Coventry. Several
children were the issue of this marriage, one
of whom, Gervase, was born in the year 1568.
The early years of Gervase Kirke were spent

1 William Blythe, of Norton, had a grant of arms in the reign of
Henry VII. [1485]. The arms are, "*Ermine*, three roebucks, trippant,
gules, attired, *or*." This William Blythe was father of the two bishops.
The monument of William Blythe and his wife, and another of their
eldest son, Richard, are in Norton Church. They were erected by
Bishop Geoffrey Blythe, who founded a chantry for the souls of his
parents. In 1524 he agreed with the parish to give ten marks for
the purpose of keeping up a stock of ten kine, in consideration of a
little croft on the West Side of Norton Green, on which he built the
Chantry Chapel. The Vicar was bound to keep up the stock of kine,
in default of which he was to forfeit the corrody of nine gallons of
ale, and nine keysts of bread, which he received weekly from
Beauchief Abbey.

C

in his father's house at Norton,[1] a quiet village
in the extreme north of Derbyshire, where
the great questions which were at that time
shaking the heart of England, found but a
feeble echo: a pleasant place though in its
own way, with an ancient church, not long
before one of the cherished possessions of the
monks of Beauchief, the Abbey itself lying
but a little way off, unroofed and owl-haunted,
but still beautiful. No longer could mass be
sung in the Abbey de Bello Capite,[2] for the
soul of the founder, Thomas de Alfreton, once
a murderer of the martyred Thomas of
Canterbury; let us hope that his crime has
been expiated by the prayers of four hundred
years. But, quiet and retired as it was,
Norton could not remain ignorant of the plots

1 Norton afterwards became celebrated as the birthplace of the
sculptor Chantrey, who was born at Jordanthorpe, a small cottage
in this parish, on the 7th April, 1781. His bones now rest in the
churchyard; and by his will he left £5 per annum to ten poor boys
of the village of Norton, so long as they will pluck the weeds and
nettles from his grave.

2 Beauchief Abbey was founded by Thomas de Alfrèton about
the year 1176. Norton Church was granted to the Abbey by its
founder.

and dark doings which were hatching in the
country, especially in Derbyshire, where the
chief object of all these dealings was residing
as a guest,[1] rather than a captive. Chatsworth
is not far from Norton, and the fascinations
which in a little time roused the wild passions
of Babington and his fellows, may have excited some feeling in the quiet country village,
and led men to think what would be the
end of these things. During the Queen of
Scots' residence in Derbyshire, Gervase Kirke
was not yet of an age to be influenced by
her wrongs; and far other thoughts as to his
prospects in life were entertained for him by
his father than that he should connive at
treason, which could only bring him to a

1 As a proof of Lord Shrewsbury's kind treatment of the Queen
of Scots, see a letter written by Mrs. Battell, a gentlewoman to the
Countess of Shrewsbury, to the Lady Elizabeth Powlett, at Clerken-
well, dated March 23rd, 1584, and preserved in the Record Office, in
which she complains of "her lord's hard dealing towards her in consequence of the Queen of Scots not being able to abide her; the said
Scottish Queen having conceived this dislike to her through Mrs.
Battell having said of her, that it was fitter she should be hanged
than ever be Queen of England. If her lord continues his hard
speech she cannot abide it no longer, and one of her chief offences is
that she pities her mistress."

cruel and bloody death. At an early age he
was sent to London, and bound apprentice
to a merchant in that city.

Commerce was at this time the ruling
passion in England. The marriage of Anjou
with the Queen, the troubles in Scotland, the
balance of power in Europe, might fill the
minds of Elizabeth and her ministers; the
murder of the English, and the release of the
Scottish Queen, might be seething in the
brains of a few desperate and bigoted men,
but the majority of the English nation cared
for none of these things. The Prince of
Orange, struggling for religious freedom
against overwhelming odds, received but cold
acknowledgment; but when Philip of Spain
threatened to retaliate upon English shipping
the losses sustained from Drake in America,
half London was clamouring at the doors of
the Council board. And we must not revile
them for such feelings: to the majority of
Englishmen the Prince of Orange was a rebel,
and the Hollanders were but rivals in maritime

commerce; whilst alliance with Spain meant trade with the richest country in the world, and plentiful employment of English ships, which at this time monopolized the greater part of the northern carrying trade. True, that English sailors sometimes made acquaintance with the inside of Spanish prisons, and felt the tender embraces of the Inquisition; but great gains are not to be had without some risk.

At the accession of Elizabeth, England had awakened to a new life. Sacerdotalism was extinct, monkery was dead, all example and precept for idleness had disappeared; the dissolution of the monasteries had conferred wealth upon the aristocracy; immunity from taxation enriched the state of the burgher and peasant. The country rejoiced to live under a Queen, thrifty and penurious, who lived upon her income, and disliking a Parliament, managed to do without subsidies. Majestic houses arose on the estates of the nobles; lands were enclosed and villenage disappeared. Merchants

and manufacturers, the latter attracted from
abroad in search of that freedom of thought
which their own country denied them, grew
and prospered under a monarch who was herself a trader; and who considered, wisely
enough, that to get money by trade was better
than to spend it in war. But foremost in the
causes which helped to forward the develop-
ment of English commerce, must be placed
the discovery of America. It may seem ab-
surd to mention the discovery of America in
the latter half of the sixteenth century, but
it is nevertheless true that America was not
truly discovered by England until that time.
It seems almost incredible that, after the discovery of North America by John Cabot, in
1491, seventy-two years elapsed before any
attempt was made to utilize that discovery,
which opened such a vast territory to English
enterprise and capital; but the domestic
troubles of Henry VIII.'s reign, and the
religious differences under Edward VI. and
Mary—reigns peculiarly adverse to the exten-

sion of industry, trade, and navigation—had
intervened to check all attempts at surveying
the coasts, or colonizing the territory which
Cabot and his sons had discovered. Spain
alone at this time was reaping a rich harvest
from America, and yearly vast treasure-ships
sailed across the Atlantic to empty into her
bosom the spoils of a new continent. English
sailors lying in the Tagus or Guadalquiver
heard of these rich lands across the sea; saw
the advent of rich argosies, deep in the sea
with freight of gold and silver in solid bars,
measured at once Spain's wealth and weakness
with their hunger and strength, and determined to share in such a goodly trade. In
the Thames and the Avon, off Plymouth and
Dartmouth, many a bold seaman felt his mouth
water over the accounts of Spanish wealth,
and was quite ready to exchange iron for gold,
cold round shots for shining yellow ingots.
Many Englishmen had already visited Spanish
America, a few voluntarily, but others as
galley slaves, condemned by the Inquisition;

and strange tales were told by such of them
as returned home, of the wealth and beauty of
that distant land, and the fiendish cruelty of
the Spaniards; till between hunger for gold
and hatred of the Inquisition every English-
man was eager to undertake an expedition to
America. The whole country awoke to a
new life; wonderful accounts of the newly
discovered regions were narrated at village
crosses; all the gossips of our market towns
were agape for new wonders, which we
may be sure did not lose by repetition;
and strange tales indeed were told about
these unknown regions. Travellers reported
at large upon the dress and habits of
of the people who inhabited them, the women
"wearing great plates of gold covering their
whole body like armour;" of their god, as
a devil who appeared in the likeness of a
calf; the soil most excellent; animals and
birds in great number, some "great beasts as
big as two of our oxen;" of their treasures,
"pearls in every house, in some houses a

peck." Besides these, other travellers described[1] "banqueting houses built of crystal, with pillars of massive silver, some of gold;" pieces of clear gold as big as a man's fist. These and other such tales were received with credulous delight. Here was El Dorado, where a man could fill his pockets with gold! With such dreams as these the English nation gave itself up to trade and discovery. Younger sons of county gentry who had no hope to share in the division of the paternal acres, flocked to London or Bristol, to learn a trade and share in the rich prizes which a mercantile career now offered. Many a rich and noble family was founded at this time by merchants of London; and it does not follow because they were merchants they were not men of gentle blood. If we look through the visitation of London, taken by St. George in 1634, we shall find that more than half the eminent merchants whose pedigrees are there entered, were the grandsons of country gentlemen entitled to wear coat armour.

1 Colonial Papers. Vol. I. No. 2.

The spirit of commercial enterprise which had been awakened under Mary, seemed to pervade and animate every description of men during the reign of Elizabeth. For the extension of trade and the discovery of unknown lands associations were formed, companies were incorporated, expeditions were planned; and the prospect of immense profit, which though always anticipated was seldom realized, seduced many to sacrifice their whole fortunes, prevailed even upon the ministers, the nobility, and the Queen herself to risk considerable sums in their hazardous undertakings. In 1583, Drake made his celebrated voyage, circumnavigated the globe, and returned with a vast treasure to England, part of which the Queen appropriated to her own use, and appeared in public wearing an emerald cross, part of Drake's robberies. In vain the Spanish government demanded redress for this and other spoliations. Elizabeth filled her coffers and evaded all demands. Philip's patience was at last worn out, and the Armada was the only practical answer to Drake's piracies. By the destruction of the great fleet the seas were thrown open to English ships; the war became offensive instead of defensive, and the English flag flaunted at the same time off Cadiz and Carthagena.

The conclusion of the Spanish war turned public attention in England from South to North America. The former had been acquired by Spain and Portugal; why should not the latter become an appanage of the English crown? Several expeditions had been made to North America in the reign of Elizabeth, but none of these had been productive of any great results: but after the accession of James I., several companies of adventurers were incorporated to trade and colonize in North America. Of these merchant adventurers Gervase Kirke was one of the first and most active. He had served out his apprenticeship in London, and having been in business for some time on his own account, was, at the commencement of the 17th century,

a wealthy and influential citizen. About the
year 1596, he had married Elizabeth, daughter
of M. Goudon, of Dieppe, in France, by
whom he had five sons and two daughters.[1]

The Company of Merchant Adventurers
of London, joined by Gervase Kirke, fitted
out ships, and sent them to take part in the
fish and fur trade of America. In these enterprises David Kirke and his two younger
brothers were at an early age associated, and
they made several cruises in the Company's
ships. In the year 1627, a Company was
formed by Sir William Alexander, Gervase
Kirke, and others, to form a settlement in
Canada for the purpose of trading with the
natives. To assist them to this end, they
obtained a patent from the King of England,
appointing them sole commissioners for making
a voyage to the gulf and river of Canada and
parts adjacent, with authority to settle a plan-

1 David Kirke, his eldest son, born in the year 1597; and Lewis
Kirke, second son, born in 1599; Thomas, third son, born 1603; John,
fourth son, born 1606; and James, born 1616; Elizabeth, his eldest
daughter, who afterwards married M. Jacques Gretemlaw, a Frenchman
of Dieppe; and Mary, youngest daughter, born in 1619.

tation, with a prohibition to all others to trade there. Power was granted by this patent to seize French and Spanish vessels and goods, and to displace the French if possible.[1]

Before we can understand the events which took place upon Captain Kirke's arrival in Canada, it will be necessary to consider what position the French held in that country and Nova Scotia at the time of his voyage; and to do so satisfactorily will entail a brief narrative of the different settlements effected in that country from its discovery by Cartier to the year 1627.

Jacques Cartier was a master mariner, of St. Malo, who was sent on a mission of discovery by Chabot, Admiral of France, for the purpose of establishing a colony upon the newly-discovered continent of America. He sailed from St. Malo on the 20th of April, 1534, with two vessels, neither of which was above twenty tons burden, arrived at Newfoundland, near Cape Bonavista, on the

1 See Appendix D. Also Colonial Papers. Vol. IV. No. 23.

10th of May, and then traversed the coast to
the South, landing at a harbour which he
named St. Catherine. Proceeding North West,
he entered the Gulf of St. Lawrence and
passed in sight of an island which he called
"Isle des Oiseaux." After cruising about the
west coast of Newfoundland, he crossed into a
deep inlet which he called "Bay de Chaleur,"
on account of the great heat caused by the summer weather when he entered it. After exploring this bay he returned to France, and
arrived at St. Malo on the 15th of September.
In the following year, owing to his favourable
report of the country and climate, Cartier was
put in command of three ships of superior
size, and well fitted out with necessaries. He
embarked on board "La Grande Hermione,"
the largest of the three, and set sail on the
19th of May. On the 26th of July, the three
ships, which had been separated by a storm,
met at an appointed rendezvous in the Gulf
of St. Lawrence, and proceeded up the river
of the same name. On the 1st of August,

Cartier was driven into a harbour on the north coast, which he called St. Nicholas. He then went on till he came to the Saghunny, from which he continued his course till his ship, the Hermione, grounded on the shoals in the Lake of St. Peter.

With two boats he explored the river to the island on which Montreal now stands, which was then inhabited by a Huron tribe who received Cartier with kindness and hospitality. Returning from this island, he came to a river which still bears his name, where he wintered. During the winter his crew suffered much from scurvy, which the natives taught him to cure by means of a decoction prepared from the bark of a kind of fir. Next summer he returned to France, and gave a most favourable report of the country and its inhabitants.[1] In January, 1540, Francois de la Roche, Seiqueur de Roberval, received a patent from Francis I. declaring him Seigneur of Norembega (a name by which nearly all North

[1] Macgregor's Hist. of British America. Vol. II. p. 329.

America was then designated), Viceroy and
Lieutenant-General of Canada, Terre Neuf,
Belle Isle, Labrador, &c., with all power and
authority possessed by the King in those
places.

It is amusing in this part of European history to see what vast districts the Kings of
England, France, and Spain granted to their
subjects; territories, the limits of which had
never been defined, and of whose existence
in many cases doubt might exist; and yet
they were granted in all formality under the
royal hand and seal, to be discovered and
conquered by the grantees at their own expense. These grants cost nothing to the
grantor but the expense of wax and parchment, and brought considerable sums in to
the royal exchequer.

Under the authority of this imposing grant,
M. de la Roche sailed to America in the summer of 1540,[1] having under his command five

1 M. de Roberval was a native of Picardy, and was recalled to
France by the King, to use his arms and influence in the war then
raging in that province.

ships, with Jacques Cartier as his Admiral.
The voyage to America was accomplished
successfully, and a fort was erected on the
mainland. The spot, however, on which it
was built proved unfortunate; it was exposed
to severe cold and hostile Indians; so Cartier,
who had been left in command, finding the
place untenable, and despairing of La Roche's
return, deserted the place, and embarked with
all his people, intending to return to France.
However, he fell in with M. de la Roche on
the banks of Newfoundland, with some ships
carrying arms and stores; so, returning with
him he resumed command of the garrison.
De la Roche sailed up the St. Lawrence as
far as Tadousac, but as to the result of
his voyage we have no reliable statement.[1]
However, nothing seems to have been done,
as some time elapsed before France sent out
another expedition.

1 M. de Roberval and his brother are said to have made another
expedition to Canada in 1545. They were called by Francis I. the one
"le gendarme d' Annibal," and the other "le petit roi de Vixeneux."
Both are said to have perished in this last expedition.

D

In the year 1598, the Marquis de la Roche left France, by order of Henry IV., to colonize Nova Scotia, carrying with him about 200 convicts from the French prisons. He landed at the Isle de Sable, situated about fifty leagues to the S.E. of Cape Breton. This island, which is almost desert, producing nothing fit for food, either animal or vegetable, was foolishly selected by the Marquis as a fit place for a settlement. Here he left forty persons, and sailed to Nova Scotia; but after cruising about for some time, and meeting with very unfavourable weather, he was compelled to return to France. The unfortunate people who were left on the Isle of Sable, were reduced to the extremity of want: without food or clothing, with no wood to form any shelter from the extreme cold, they must most inevitably have perished, had not a French ship been wrecked on the island, and a few sheep washed on shore; with the boards of the wreck they constructed huts to shelter themselves from the cold, but the sheep were soon eaten, and they were compelled to live wholly on fish. They clothed themselves in the skins of seals, and in this wretched state spent seven years. Fortunately, they had not been altogether forgotten, for King Henry IV. ordered Chetodel, who had been M. de la Roche's pilot, to bring them back to France. When Chetodel arrived at the Island, he found only twelve men alive, with whom he returned to France; and their squalid and miserable appearance in their sealskin clothes and long beards so moved the King's compassion that he gave them a general pardon for all their offences, and presented each of them with fifty crowns. De la Roche must have been ignorant of the condition of the Isle of Sable, or he never would have attempted to form a settlement there. This dismal place, celebrated only for the number of wrecks which occur on its coasts, is a bare, sandy desert, without tree or shrub of any kind, larger than bilberry bushes, and producing no food, except cranberries, which grow in

abundance. Continual storms sweep over it,
and often the whole face of the country is
altered in a single night, by the shifting of
the sand hills of which it is composed. Earth-
quakes are frequent, altering the coast line,
throwing up reefs, and so making navigation
still more dangerous in its vicinity. Efforts
at cultivation have hitherto failed, though by
unceasing care a cabbage has been known to
attain maturity.

In 1600 and 1601, M. de Chauvin made
two voyages to Tadousac, and returned to
France laden with furs, which he sold at a
great profit. When just starting upon another
expedition, he suddenly died. But these
voyages of M. de Chauvin bore fruit; the
large sum of money realized by him and his
brother adventurers, stirred up an extraordinary spirit of enterprise amongst the French
merchants.

In 1603, M. de Monts, a French Protestant,
and a gentleman of a resolute and enterprising
spirit, obtained a patent from Henry IV. for

"inhabiting Acadia, Canada, and other places
in New France." He was constituted the
King's Lieutenant-General "for to represent
our person in the countries, territories, coasts,
and confines of La Cadia, from the 40 to the
46 degree;"[1] his patent also granted him
the exclusive right to traffic in furs, so that
a great number of wealthy men were on that
account induced to join in the adventure.
De Monts soon fitted out and equipped four
ships, laden with all necessaries and goods,
and in March, 1604, sailed from Havre, De
Monts himself having the chief command,
accompanied by Champlain, as pilot, and M.
Potrincourt and M. Champdore, two personal
friends, with several other gentlemen of position. De Monts, being a Protestant, had obtained permission for the free exercise of his
religion within his goverment. On the 15th
of May, 1604, he arrived at a harbour
on the S.E. of Acadia, known now by the
name of Liverpool, where finding a French

1 Colonial Papers. Vol. I. No. 10.

trader, named Rossignol, trading for furs
without a license, he confiscated the vessel
and cargo, naming the harbour Port Rossignol, as if to compensate the wretched man
for the loss of his property. De Monts then
sailed westward to Port Mouton (so called
from a sheep leaping overboard at that spot),
where he landed and formed an encampment,
by erecting wigwams after the manner of
the Indians.

The vessels under De Monts having different
destinations, the one which carried the principal supplies for the winter, commanded by
M. Morell, and which had been ordered to
proceed to Canseau, not having been heard
of, De Monts thought it better to stop at
Cape Mouton, until the missing vessel should
arrive. Here they remained a month, fishing,
hunting, and making excursions into the
country, but the reduced state of their provisions, and the continued absence of Morell,
filled them with alarm and anxiety. The
missing vessel not only contained food for

the winter, but also axes and tools for building, so that it would have been impossible
either to winter there or to return to France,
unless it arrived quickly. However, in a few
days after the month, De Monts heard of the
safe arrival of Morell at Canseau: it appears
that he had been delayed by confiscating four
French ships, that he had found trading for
furs without a license. De Monts soon afterwards dispatched this ship to Tadousac, after
having discharged its cargo: the two other
vessels were ordered to cruise along the shore
of Cape Breton and Acadia, to prevent un-
authorised trading with the natives. From
thence De Monts, in his own ship, coasted the
peninsula to the south-west, doubled Cape
Sable, and anchored in the Bay of St. Mary,
where he discovered some iron ore, and also
a mineral containing a small proportion of
silver. He traversed the Bay of Fundy, and
by a narrow strait entered a beautiful and
spacious basin, surrounded by hills clothed
with luxuriant woods, from which streams of

limpid water descended into the lake. Potrincourt was so charmed with the beauty and
fertility of this place, that he requested M.
de Monts to make him a grant of it, and
soon afterwards returned to France to bring
his family, and settle in this lovely place,
which he called Port Royal.

From this place De Monts sailed further
into the Bay of Fundy, and discovered a copper mine at a place now called Cape D'Or.
He also discovered a great river which the
natives called Onangondy, but which he named
St. John, as it was discovered on the 24th of
June, the festival of St. John the Baptist.
They sailed up this river as far as they could,
and found its banks clothed with trees, grapes
growing wild, its waters filled with fish, and
the whole scenery varied and beautiful. From
this river they coasted south-westerly, until
they came to another river, called St. Croix,
on a small island at the entrance to which
De Monts commenced forming a settlement
by clearing trees, erecting a fort, a church,

and several houses. The place was badly
chosen, as it afforded neither fresh water nor
food for the winter, and out of the whole
seventy-six who composed De Monts' colony
thirty-seven died of scurvy brought on by
eating salt meat and drinking melted snow.
The savages inhabiting the neighbouring islands and shores assembled at St. Croix,
visited the French in their encampment, and
were charmed with their society and manners.

Finding St. Croix unhealthy and otherwise
unsuited for a permanent settlement, De Monts
determined to abandon it in the spring, and
with that intent he explored the west side of
the island in the hope of finding some place
to which he could remove. Disappointed in
his search, he determined to sail for Newfoundland, and then return to France; but
whilst he was making preparations for his
voyage, Pontgrave arrived with supplies and
a reinforcement of forty men, and at his sugges-
tion the whole party moved to Port Royal.[1]

1 Now called Annapolis.

Here they established themselves; built a fort
and magazine, and having housed all their
stores found themselves comfortably settled.
As autumn advanced De Monts sailed for
France, leaving Pontgrave, Champdore, and
Champlain in command of the colony. During
the winter the settlement was plentifully supplied with venison, but there was a great
scarcity of bread.

De Monts and Potrincourt were in the
meanwhile preparing in France for another
expedition. On the 13th of May, 1606, they
sailed from Honfleur in a vessel of 150 tons,
and after a long voyage arrived at Canseau,
whence they despatched a party of Indians to
announce their arrival to the settlers at Port
Royal. Pontgrave in the meanwhile had
attempted to explore the coast south of Cape
Cod, but was driven back and shipwrecked
near the entrance to Port Royal. In consequence of this disaster he built two small
vessels, and putting all he could on board of
them, and leaving two volunteers in charge

of the stores left behind, he proceeded to
Canseau, before the arrival of the messengers
of De Monts, but returned on meeting with
a boat's crew which De Monts had left at
that place.

But with all De Monts' energy, the settlement at Port Royal would have been a failure
but for the assistance of a French gentleman,
named Lescarbot, who from personal attach-
ment had accompanied Potrincourt. He
showed the urgent necessity of making themselves independent of the Indians by import-
ing and breeding European cattle, and by
cultivating the soil. De Monts left Acadia
for France in August, 1606. Anxious to
re-establish a colony in the South he sent
Potrincourt to explore; but this, like his other
voyage, proved unsuccessful, and he returned
to Port Royal in November. During this
voyage he was attacked by the Indians, who
killed two of his men and wounded several
others. His return was celebrated with great
festivity; he was received with great for-

mality by his friends, who united in a procession and escorted him to the fort, reciting verses composed by Lescarbot for the occasion. The houses of Potrincourt and De Monts were hung with laurel and adorned with appropriate mottoes.[1]

The winter, which was mild and pleasant, was spent by the settlers in a happy manner. Their days were passed in hunting and fishing and short excursions into the country. Potrincourt, Lescarbot, Champlain, and twelve others formed themselves into a club, called Le bon temps, in which each member by turns took upon himself the duties of caterer and steward for the day. After dinner they amused themselves with music and recitations.

After waiting a long time for the return of De Monts with supplies from France, a vessel at length arrived bringing only a few provisions and stores, and conveying the mortifying news that the charter of De Monts had been cancelled, in consequence of the

1 Halliburton's Nova Scotia. Vol. I. p. 25.

remonstrances made against it by the French merchants, and that he was therefore under the necessity of abandoning all connection with Acadia. Potrincourt, distressed but not disheartened by this intelligence, determined to proceed to France and procure if possible a grant of the colony, assured that with very little assistance it must now succeed. He waited, however, till he could collect together specimens of the native produce, furs, skins, and minerals, together with samples of wheat, rye, and other grain which the colonists had grown, to lay before the French King. By these means he managed to procure a grant of Port Royal, saddled with the condition that he should take two Jesuits with him to convert the Indians. Potrincourt, who, though a Roman Catholic, had a great aversion to Jesuits, was disgusted at this arrangement, and plainly told the Jesuits when they arrived at Port Royal that they must not meddle with his affairs, but confine themselves to teaching religion. In fact, he made the place so uncomfortable for them that the two Jesuits made frequent complaints of him and his son, Biencourt. Their troubles were apparently terminated by the arrival of a vessel despatched, in 1613, by a lady, named De Guercheville. This ship, which had on board two priests, carried away the Jesuits from Port Royal, and sailing into the Bay of Fundy they fixed upon the Island of Mount Desert, where they formed a settlement. They were proceeding rapidly with their buildings, when they were surprised by an English ship from Virginia, commanded by Captain Argoll, who pillaged the place, seized the ships, and compelled them to surrender as prisoners of war, but not before one of the Jesuits had been shot through the head whilst urging the settlers to defend themselves.

This affair led to the fitting-out of an armament from Virginia under Captain Argoll, to dislodge the French from Acadia. Piloted by the Jesuit Beart, who thirsted for revenge, Argoll appeared before Port Royal, and

destroyed the fort.   Biencourt attempted to
treat with him, but the conference ended by
some of the French joining the savages,
others leaving for Quebec, and by those who
surrendered being sent to England.

This outrageous affair, committed in a time
of peace between England and France,
destroyed the first settlement made in North
America, after it had prospered for eight or
nine years.   But, though Port Royal had been
destroyed, great numbers of French and
several Dutch adventurers settled themselves
in different parts of Acadia, especially about
Canseau, where they carried on a profitable
fur trade; and, about the time of Captain
David Kirke's first expedition, were in a
very flourishing condition.

In the events which followed, Nova Scotia
was so intimately connected with Canada,
that it will be as well to trace the history of
the latter country down to this period, before
considering the effect of Kirke's expedition
upon the French settlement.   That distin-

guished navigator Champlain, who had accompanied M. de la Roche in his expedition
up the St. Lawrence, and had afterwards
joined the adventurers to Acadia, made, in
1608, another voyage up the St. Lawrence,
and established himself upon a most command-
ing promontory, situated on the north bank of
the river, and to which he gave the name of
Quebec. Here he left a few settlers, and returning next year with Pontgrave to his infant
colony, found it in quiet possession, clearing
and cultivating the ground with partial success.
Champlain explored the Ottawa and other parts
of the country before he returned to France,
where he succeeded in forming, under the
patronage of the Prince de Condè, a new asso-
ciation at Rouen. He returned to Canada in
1612, taking with him four Recollects,[1] for the
purpose of converting the savages. During
the next eight years he was engaged in war

1 The Recollects, or Recollets, were minor Friars of the Reformed
Order of St. Francis. This sect, which began in Spain, was introduced
into Italy A.D. 1525, and into France A.D. 1584, or 1592. They were
called Recollets because they professed to lead a life more austere
and more reserved than ordinary religious professors.

with the Iroquois, which took all his attention.
In 1620 he brought his family to Canada.

The Duc de Ventadour, in 1622, having
taken Holy Orders, accepted the office of
Viceroy of New France, solely with the view
of converting the savages, and for this purpose
he sent Jesuits to Canada. This was a great
mortification to the Recollects, so that incessant bickerings and quarrels arose between
them and the Roman Catholics, which came
to such a pass as seriously to retard the infant
settlement. .To put an end to these dis-
turbances the Cardinal Richelieu established
the Company of New France. This[1] Company, consisting of three hundred associates,
engaged to send three hundred tradesmen to
New France, and to supply all those who
settled in the country with lodging, food, and
clothing for three years, after which they
would grant to each workman sufficient land
to keep him, with seed to cultivate it. The
Company also engaged to have six thousand

1 Macgregor's British America. Vol. II., p. 336.

E

French inhabitants settled before 1643, and
to establish three priests in each settlement.
The prerogatives which the King reserved
for himself were, the supremacy in matters of
faith; homage as sovereign of New France;
with the acknowledgment of a crown of gold,
weighing eight marks, on each succession to
the throne of France; the nomination of all
commanders and officers of forts; and the
appointment of officers of justice, whenever
it became necessary to establish courts of law.

The Royal Charter then granted to the
Company of New France, and their successors
for ever, in consideration of their engagements
to the crown, the fort and settlement of
Quebec, all the territory of New France,
including Florida, with all the rivers along
the course of the great river of Canada, and
all other rivers which discharge themselves
therein, or which throughout these vast regions
empty themselves into the sea, both on the
East and West coasts of the Continent, with
all the harbours, islands, mines, and rights of
fishery.

The Company was further empowered to grant titles of distinction, which, however, required the confirmation of the Sovereign. The exclusive right to traffic in peltries and all other commerce, except the cod and whale fisheries, was granted to them for fifteen years. Two ships of war were given to the Company by the King, on the condition that their value should be refunded if the Company failed to send at least one thousand five hundred French people of both sexes to New France in the first ten years.

Such were the provisions of this celebrated Charter, which was signed in April, 1627. The most flattering expectations of success were raised; ships filled with stores sailed from France, numbers of eager emigrants crowded their decks; priests, fired with religious zeal, hastened to offer their services to convert the poor heathen from darkness to the light of Roman Catholicism; everything seemed to favour the colony. But all these great expectations were destined to disappointment. A small squadron of ships was being fitted out in England, under the command of Captain David Kirke, which was destined to delay considerably, it might have been for ever, the establishment of a prosperous French colony on the shores of the St. Lawrence.

CHAPTER II.

Birth and Education of Sir William Alexander—Obtains a Grant of
Nova Scotia from James I.—First English Colony in Nova Scotia—
War between England and France declared—Renewal of Sir William
Alexander's Patent by Charles I.—The Order of Nova Scotian Baronets
Founded—Sir William joins the Canada Company—Second Expedition
fitted out under the command of David Kirke, which arrives in safety
at Newfoundland—Sails up the St. Lawrence to Tadousac—Returns
to Gaspè—Meets the French Squadron, which Captain Kirke Defeats
and Captures—Reduction of Port Royal and other French Settlements
—Excitement in France—Kirke Returns to England—Third Expedition to Canada, &c., under Captain Kirke—Arrives at Gaspè—Sails up
the St. Lawrence—Defeat of M. de Caen—Kirke appears before Quebec
—Champlain's Distress—Surrender of Quebec—Return of David
Kirke to England—Peace of Versailles—Surrender of Canada and
Acadia to the French—Petition to the King—Honorary Grant of Arms
to David Kirke and his Brothers—Knighthood of David Kirke—His
Marriage.

In the year 1621, Sir William Alexander, of
Menstrie, who was a great favourite with
James I., applied to him for a grant of
Acadia. Sir William was a younger son of

Alexander Alexander, of Menstrie, and was
born in the year 1580. Having received a
liberal education he was selected as travelling
companion to the Duke of Argyll. On his
return from the continent he lived for some
time a retired life in Scotland, and published
his "Aurora," a poetical complaint upon his
unsuccessful addresses to a lady, who, declin-
ing the honour of his hand, had, as he expressed
it, "matched her morning to one in the even-
ing of his days." Not long after this he
married Janet, daughter and heiress of Sir
William Erskine, and removed to the court
of James VI., when he published a tragedy
on the story of Darius, and two poems, one
congratulating his Majesty on his entry into
England, the other on the inundation at Dover,
where the King used to amuse himself with
hawking. In 1607, his dramas, entitled "The
Monarchial Tragedies," were published, containing Darius Crœsus, the Alexandræan, and
Julius Cæsar; he was also the author of a
poem called "Doomesday," and several other

pieces, and it is said his Majesty used to call
him his philosophical poet. In 1613 he was
appointed one of the gentlemen ushers to
Prince Charles, and master of the requests,
and received the honour of knighthood. In
1621, he received the grant of Nova Scotia
as mentioned above. He had charters of the
Lordship of Canada in 1628, of the Barony of
Menstrie in the same year; Barony of Largis,
11th April, 1629; Barony of Tullibody on 30th
of July in the same year. Sworn of the Privy
Council and Secretary of State, in 1626;
Keeper of the Signet, 1627; Commissioner of
the Exchequer, 1628; one of the extraordinary
Lords of Session, 1631. Created Lord Alexander of Tullibody, Viscount Stirling, by
patent, 4th September, 1630, and Earl of
Stirling, Viscount Canada and Lord Alexander,
by patent, 14th of June, 1633. In 1637, he
was made Earl of Doban. Such was the man
who applied, in 1621, to James I. for a grant
of Nova Scotia, then called Acadia; and as
but little trouble was wanted at that time to

obtain a grant of a whole province in America,
he was gratified by a grant of the whole of
Acadia, which was named in the patent[1] Nova
Scotia. In the year after his grant in 1623,
Sir William despatched a number of emigrants
to take possession of the country, but they
got no further than Newfoundland before the
cold weather set in, which obliged them to
pass the winter there. In the following spring
they set out for Nova Scotia, and coasted
along the South shore. Here they discovered
that in the interval between the destruction
of the colony by Argoll and the grant to Sir
William, the country had been occupied not
only by the survivors of the former emigrants,
but also by adventurers from all parts, who
had increased to formidable numbers. Under
these circumstances they thought it prudent
to return to England, where, on their arrival,
they published an account of the country, in
which they boasted of fertile plains, rivers
embosomed in trees and stocked with fish,

1 Colonial Papers. Vol. IV., No. 23.

safe harbours, and a country abounding with
game of all kinds. Though these adventurers
published an account of a country which they
had never seen—not an uncommon thing at
the time in which they lived—they seem,
singularly enough, to have given a very fair
description of Nova Scotia, which then as
now was as amply supplied with all necessaries as they described it to be.

War breaking out between England and
France at this time, an opportunity was offered
for crushing the infant settlements of France
in Nova Scotia and Canada. Charles I.,
warmly patronizing Sir William Alexander,
renewed the grant of his father by a patent
dated 12th of July, 1624. He also founded
the order of Knights Baronet of Nova Scotia,
who were to contribute their aid to the settlement, upon the consideration of each having
alloted to him a liberal portion of land.
However venerable the order of English
Baronets may have become, it cannot be
denied that its creation brought little honour

either to its founder or to the first possessors
of the dignity.   Still less can the Baronets of
Nova Scotia look back with pleasure to their
first creation, however mysterious that event
may seem through lapse of time, and the
strange eccentricity that appears to have
governed their selection.   James I. created
any gentleman an English Baronet who would
maintain thirty foot soldiers in Ireland for
three years at eightpence a day each; but if
any gentleman would take a voyage to Nova
Scotia, he received a grant of land six miles
in length by three in breadth, and was made
a Baronet of Nova Scotia into the bargain.[1]
Strange as it may seem, but few responded
to this invitation, so further inducements were
held out.   Not only should any gentleman
settling in Nova Scotia be made a Baronet,
but he and his heirs male should enjoy the
privilege of wearing and " carrying about
their necks an orange tawny silk ribbon,
whereon shall hang pendant in an escutcheon

1 Banks' Baronia Anglica Concentrata.   Appendix.

argent, a saltire *azure*, thereon an escutcheon of the arms of Scotland, with an imperial crown above the escutcheon, and encircled with the motto ' Fax meritis honestæ gloria.'" In a second grant to Sir William Alexander, power was given to him to make Baronets; and his first exercise of this power was in making a Baronet of Claude de St. Etienne, *alias* Claude de la Tour, a French adventurer, equally devoid of religion and honesty, a Huguenot and a Protestant under the British Monarch, a Catholic under Louis XIV., at all times an active, enterprising, treacherous, and unscrupulous man, who made religion a stalking horse to gain the object of his ambition.

As Nova Scotia was ceded to the French in 1632, the Baronets of that country found themselves in possession of an empty title and a tawny orange ribbon. Their order came to an untimely end, but Charles II. having created some Baronets of *Scotland*, the new and the old Scotia amalgamated, and the titled of either country considered those

of the other as belonging to the same order.
A meeting of the amalgamated Baronets was
held in Edinburgh in 1774, when it was
determined to assert their right to wear the
orange tawny ribbon with its accessories.
Determinations to this effect were presented
to the King through the Earl of Suffolk, but
His Majesty took no notice of the declaration;
and although certain Scotchmen appeared at
court on St. Andrew's Day wearing the orange
ribbon, they seem soon to have abandoned
the custom, no doubt finding the colour somewhat trying to their complexions.

Backed up by the court and with visions of
wealth and grandeur floating before his eyes,
Sir William Alexander fitted out a small but
well-appointed armament in 1627. His eagerness in this expedition excited the mirth of
Buckingham and the other courtiers. "James,"
they said, "was a King who tried to be a
poet, and Alexander a poet who wished to
be a King." He was assisted by several
eminent merchants of London—chief amongst

whom was Gervase Kirke—who considered the project a good one, and were willing to embark a large sum of money in the enterprise.

In the spring of 1627,[1] the small fleet, consisting of three ships, set sail from England. The whole was under the command of Captain David Kirke, who sailed in the largest ship, a vessel of about 300 tons, whilst the other two were under the command of his brothers, Lewis and Thomas, respectively. They had obtained letters of marque from the King, under the broad seal, giving them authority to capture and destroy any French ships which they might encounter, and utterly to drive away and root out the French settlements in Nova Scotia and Canada.

After a favourable voyage across the Atlantic, Kirke arrived in safety at Newfoundland, where he resolved to wait for a short time, until he should receive information about the French. Before leaving England he had

1 Halliburton's Nova Scotia. Vol. I., p. 43.

heard rumours of a great armament fitting
out in France to establish the New Company
in Canada, and he was anxious to ascertain
the number and size of the ships which composed the squadron daily expected off the
coast of Nova Scotia.

In the meanwhile, great eagerness had been
shown in France to furnish supplies and ammunition to their colony at Quebec. Twenty
vessels were laden with stores, food, building
implements, guns, and ammunition; nearly
150 pieces of ordnance were stowed away in
the different holds to be mounted upon the
walls of Quebec and other forts; the decks
were crowded with emigrants, male and
female; priests were there, burning with religious zeal; and everything looked hopeful
for their success. The whole fleet was put
under the command of M. de Roquemont, a
French Admiral; and full of hope and expectation they set sail from France in the
month of April, 1627.

Whilst they were on their way across the

Atlantic, Captain Kirke, tired of waiting,
sailed from Newfoundland, and visiting the
French settlements in the neighbourhood of
Cape Tourmente, destroyed all the houses
and forts which had been erected there. He
then sailed up the St. Lawrence as far as
Tadousac, but hearing at that place that M.
de Roquemont had not arrived but was daily
expected, he turned back and sailed down the
river, hoping to fall in with the squadron.
He was not disappointed, for upon doubling
Gaspè point he saw the whole French squadron,
which had taken refuge in the bay from a
violent storm. It was a critical moment for
both commanders. On the one hand M. de
Roquemont, though far superior in number
of ships and men, was well aware that he
was in no condition to fight; his ships were
laden heavily with stores, and though he had
150 cannon on board, they were lying in the
different holds and were of no use, whilst the
number he had for service were very few and
of small calibre. His ships were deep in the

water and rather unmanageable; his decks
were crowded with priests and non-combatants
besides women and children, who, in case of
a fight, would be exposed to terrible danger.
On the other hand the enemy had only three
ships; for all he knew they were as much
encumbered with stores and emigrants as he
was, and it was a hard case to give up the
cause of the colony almost within sight of
their destination without firing a shot or striking a blow for its sake. So he resolved to
fight. Captain Kirke on his side, though well
aware how unprepared De Roquemont was
for a combat, hesitated to attack so formidable
a force with his own three ships; but though
few in number, they were armed to the teeth,
equipped not for commerce, but for hard
fighting, and the prize was too great to be
allowed to slip through their fingers without
a struggle. But first, to spare bloodshed, he
sent a polite message to M. de Roquemont
informing him of his commission from the
King of England and summoning him to

surrender. De Roquemont returned a spirited refusal; upon receiving which David Kirke and his two brothers bore down upon the French squadron. David Kirke, sailing under the stern of the French Admiral's ship, delivered a broadside, then rounding too, threw out grappling irons and boarded: the resistance was trifling, and in a few minutes Kirke was master of the ship. His brothers at the same time captured two other ships, and the rest, being mostly sloops filled with guns and stores, seeing that their Admiral was captured, surrendered at discretion. His prizes were so numerous that his very success placed Captain Kirke in a difficulty. He counted eighteen sail all filled with stores and implements, and no less than 138 pieces of cannon. So having rifled ten of the smaller ships he set them on fire, and filling the remainder with the most valuable stores sent them to Newfoundland. He himself, with his brothers, after reducing Port Royal and other French stations on the north coast of Nova Scotia, returned to Eng-

F

land, having on board M. de Roquemont,
M. de la Tour, and other Frenchmen of distinction; and in their holds the 138 cannon
which they had taken from the French.[1]
When the news of this disaster reached M.
Champlain at Quebec, he was in despair.
Almost without provisions, hemmed in by
the Iroquois on every side, the wretched
colonists were reduced to the verge of destruction: all their hopes had been centred upon
the arrival of the squadron from France, and
now they were doomed to disappointment.
Great was the fury of the French King and
Council when the news of this disaster arrived
in Paris; the merchants who had become
associates in the New Company were clamorous
for revenge; and in a solemn Council, held by
the King, Captain David Kirke and his
brothers were declared public enemies, and
were condemned to be burnt[2] in effigy. On

1 Colonial Papers; Vol. V., No. 34, 35, and 36. Domestic Correspondence; Car. I., Dec. 1, 1863. Appendix A. Macgregor's British
America; Vol. II., p. 338.

2 Col. Papers: Vol. V., No. 37, 49; Vol. VI., 12.

the same day, amidst the tolling of bells, three stuffed figures, representing David, Lewis, and Thomas Kirke, were carried in procession through the streets of Paris, and then burnt to ashes in the Place de Grêve amidst the yells of an exulting populace.

Such was the commencement of the struggle between England and France for supremacy in North America; a struggle extended over more than a hundred years. A lasting peace had been proclaimed between England and Spain; English pirates were no longer abetted by their government in attacks upon Spanish commerce; English adventurers must have perished for sheer want of adventure, had not North America afforded a vast field for their energies in its boundless expanse of sea and land. But their new explorations brought them face to face with their old enemies, ready to maintain by force of arms what they had already acquired, and eager to try whether the victors of Cressy and Agincourt were as invincible in the New World as in the Old.

We have seen the result of the first struggle.
Nova Scotia and Cape Breton were added to
the possessions of the English Crown; Gervase Kirke and his fellow adventurers were
enriched by the spoils taken in the ships, and
by the ransom of the prisoners; and both
parties were inflamed, the one by success, the
other by revenge, to make still greater efforts
for the possession of the North American
Colonies.

Whilst the Paris populace were shouting
and gesticulating, Captain Kirke was fitting
out, at the expense of his father, Gervase,
and Sir William Alexander, another fleet of
ships, more numerous and better equipped
than the last, intending this time to make a
clean sweep of the French settlements. Enriched by the spoil they had taken from the
French and the ransom of their prisoners, the
Canada merchants were determined to spare
no expense to render their new fleet as completely equipped as possible. Some time
elapsed in preparations, and it was not till

the middle of March, 1629, that the fleet was
ready for sea. It consisted of the "Abigail,"
Captain David Kirke, 300 tons; the "William,"
Captain Lewis Kirke, 200 tons; the "George,"
Captain Thomas Kirke, 200 tons, the "Gervase," Captain Brewerton, 200 tons; besides
two other ships and three pinnaces all well
manned and armed, and furnished with letters
of marque under the broad seal of England.
With these good ships Captain Kirke left
Gravesend on the 25th of March, and after
a prosperous voyage arrived at Great Caspè
on the 15th of June. Here he divided his
force, ordering his brothers to visit the Nova
Scotian settlements and afterwards to meet
him at Tadousac. He himself in the "Abigail," accompanied by another ship, sailed up
the St. Lawrence to Tadousac, intending to
make that place his head-quarters and place
of rendezvous in his subsequent operations.
Whilst sailing up the St. Lawrence he was
attacked by a French ship under the command
of Emery de Caen, son of William de Caen,

Lord of La Motte and General of the French troops in Canada. A running fight was kept up by the " Abigail " and the French ship for several hours, at the end of which time De Caen, losing one of his masts, was disabled and obliged to surrender. In this action Captain Kirke lost three men killed, and about twenty severely wounded; the French loss was somewhat greater.[1] Having secured his prisoners and burnt the enemy's ship, Captain Kirke sailed to Tadousac, and there awaited the remainder of his fleet. Tadousac harbour lies at the mouth of the Saghunny, it is well sheltered, sufficiently deep, and affords excellent anchorage, so it was well suited for the English fleet to lie there. He did not wait long; in a few days he was joined by his brothers, when, leaving the greater part of his fleet at Tadousac, he himself, with the " George " and the " Gervase," sailed up the St. Lawrence, and appeared before Quebec on the 9th of July.

1 Col. Papers : Vol. VI., No. 15.

The capture of the stores intended for Quebec had reduced M. Champlain and his colony to the utmost distress. The prosperity of New France was not only retarded, but even the powerful mind of Champlain, so fertile in expedients on occasions of difficulty, was quite paralyzed by unfortunate circumstances and continual mortifications. The hostility of the savages was not the least of the evils that perplexed him; and the Iroquois soon perceived the advantages which the continued jealousies and quarrels between the Catholics and Huguenots enabled them to obtain over men whom they considered unwarranted occupiers of their country. Owing to their hostility, and the impossibility of communicating with France, Champlain was reduced to the utmost extremity, by the want of every article of food, clothing, implements, and ammunition; so that when Captain Kirke appeared before Quebec, the place, despite its impregnable position, was so badly victualled as to be unable to endure a siege of many days duration. If it had been well victualled and supplied with ammunition, Captain Kirke would have found it impossible, even with a much stronger force than that under his command, to subdue it. It was to the immortal credit of Champlain to have selected such a place for his settlement. Situated upon the summit of an abrupt cliff three hundred and fifty feet high, whose base is washed by a deep and rapid river, Quebec is almost unrivalled for the strength and beauty of its position. But little good was this impregnable position to its commander, when, after a few days' bombardment, he found his food exhausted, his ammunition running low, his men dying of disease and hunger, and no prospect of relief from any quarter. Under these circumstances, having done all that a brave man could do, M. Champlain sent in his submission and offered to surrender upon the following terms:

1. That Captain Kirke should show his commission from the English King.

2. That Captain Kirke may come and cast anchor before Quebec for the safety of his ships, but he shall not quit any of them to set foot on shore before he has shewn his authority.

3. To be allowed a ship to take all their company to France; Friars, Jesuits, and two savages, also their weapons, baggage, &c.

4. To have sufficient victuals in exchange for skins.

5. Favourable treatment for all.

6. To have possession of the ship three days after their arrival at Tadousac. The ship to carry about a hundred persons, some of those already captured, and some that are in this place.

These terms were submitted to Captain Kirke, and with some little alteration agreed to by him, and the following agreement was drawn up:[1]

1 Col. Papers : Vol. V., Nos. 16, 20, 33, 34.

"Articles granted to the Sieurs Champlain and De Pont by Thomas Kirke, and ratified by David Kirke. Thomas has not the King's Commission; but his brother, David, will show it to them at Tadousac. He has full powers to treat. Cannot give them a vessel, but guarantees a passage for the savages. They will be allowed to go out with their arms, clothes, baggage, and skins; the soldiers with their clothes and a beaver coat each. Skins will be exchanged for victuals. These articles will be ratified by David Kirke, the General of the Fleet."

Upon these terms M. Champlain surrendered Quebec to the English on the 9th of August, 1629. Captain Kirke treated his prisoners with such kindness that many of the poor Frenchmen and half castes chose to stay under his command at Quebec rather than undergo the horrors of an Atlantic passage. To prove to what straits they had been reduced in Quebec, the English only found one tub filled with roots (perhaps potatoes),

and no other provisions. As to the armament
of the Fort at the time of its capture the
following deposition of Champlain gives the
fullest information.

"9th November, 1629.

"Samuel Champlain, of Bromage, in Guienne,
in the Kingdom of France, Gentleman, and
late Lieutenant-Governor of the Fort of St.
Louis, at Quebec, sworne before the Right
Worshipful Sir Henry Martin, Knight, Judge
of the High Court of Admiralty, as followeth:

"That he and the rest of the French taken
at Canada, by Captain Kirke and his company, have been well used and treated by him
and his company, and since they were taken
by them giving them victuals and using them
as himselfe, and they have been noe ways
dealt with to depose an untruth for ought he
knoweth. That he was in the fort when
Captain Kirke and his company tooke the
same, and there were there in that forte and
habitation thereof, four brasse pieces each
weighing about 150 lbs. weight, one other

piece of brasse ordinance weighing eighty lbs.
weight, five iron boxes of shott for the five
brasse peeces of ordinance, two small iron
peeces of ordinance weighing each eight cwt.,
six murderers with their double boxes or
chargers, one small peece of ordinance
weighing about eighty lbs., forty-five small
iron bullets for the service of the foresaid, five
brasse peeces, six iron bullets for the service
of the foresaid, twenty-six brasse peeces weighing only three lbs. each, thirty or forty lbs.
of gunpowder all belonging to M. de Caen,
of Dieppe; about thirty lbs. of match belonging to the French King; thirteen whole and
one broken muskett, a harquebush, two large
harquebusses five or six foote longe, a peece
belonging to the Kinge, five or six thousand
leaden bulletts, plate and bars of lead belonging, sixty corseletts whereof two are compleat
and pistoll proof, two great brasse peeces
weighing eighty lbs., one pavilion to lodge
about twenty men belonging to the Kinge, a
smith's fordge with appurtenances, all neces-

saries for a carpenter, all appurtenances of ironworke for a windmill, a handmill to grind corne, a brasse bell belonging to the said merchants, and about 2,500 or 3,000 beaver skins in the magazines, and some cases of knives, and the forte belonging to the Kinge, and the habitations and houses then belong-inge to the said merchants were all left stand-ing, and the inhabitants in these houses had some goods of their owne in them, but what they were he cannot expresse.

"That there were not ane victualls or or-dinarie sustenance for men in the said forte at the time of taking it, the men in the same having lived by the space of two months before upon nothing but rootes."

It was no wonder that Champlain surren-dered. What could be expected from men who had been living for some time like swine upon roots? Cannon and ammunition they seem to have had in abundance, not to mention the murderers, which sound alarming, but it is hard work fighting upon a few roots per diem.

Thus at the end of two years from the grant of his commission by the King, Captain Kirke had destroyed all the French settlements in Canada and Nova Scotia, and annexed the whole of those vast territories to the crown of Great Britain.

To the unfortunate men his prisoners, Kirke behaved with the greatest humanity and kindness. Those of them who wished to stay in Canada he took under his protection, fed and clothed them; for the rest, who wished to return to Europe, he provided a ship of 250 tons—although it had been expressly agreed when Quebec surrendered that he should not provide any ship—and manning this ship with seventy of his own sailors, he conveyed more than a hundred of them to England, providing them with clothes, and feeding them for seven months. So well were General de Caen and Champlain treated that they began to fear they were running up too large a bill, and actually refused some of the rich food that was provided for them.[1] The

1 Col. Papers : Vol. V., Nos. 33, 34.

account of their treatment cannot be better
shewn than by quoting De Caen's own statement before the Judge of the Admiralty Court.

"The General of the French, taken by
Captain Kirke, in Canada, doth acknowledge
all good usage in respect of diett and lodging.

"His grievances are—

"1. That friends and assistants have not
free accesse to him.

"2. That he is upon a diett where he hath
much more than he desires, without any
agreement what he must pay for it, which
makes him afraid that if he should long continue as he doth he should not be able to
give satisfaction for it; whereupon being asked
whie he did not take his diett with the
Maister of the house, who had divers times
invited him, offering him the freedom of his
house and garden, he answered that he loved
his private. And being further demanded
whie he did not expresse himselfe in that
point of his diett, the charge whereof he
feared, he answered that he tooke what they

brought him. And being againe demanded whether he had not cleane linnen as was fitt, or that any that would have brought him cleane linnen had been refused to come to him, he answered that he had his linnen washed in the house, but in support of the charge he desired to have a laundresse of his own, whereupon asking of the Maister of the house whie he did refuse it, he said that his house had been much troubled with two women that came thither, and having some suspicion of them he refused them entrance.

"3. The third grievance is that he is de-tayned for a ransom that neither ought to be demanded nor is he able to pay, for he holds himselfe to be noe lawful prisoner of warre, not having beene taken in warre, but upon a plantation; and he insists much upon this, that all prisoners taken on both sides since the warre between the Crownes have been freely delivered, not only those that have been taken by the King's armies and fleets, but such as have been taken upon

letters of marque, whereof he gives instance
in some taken in Newfoundland, and insists
upon the freedom that Captain Kirke gave
to all the rest that were under his command.
And for his ransome he professes his whole
estate in France is not worth about £700
sterling, and wisheth for their satisfaction
they would send over some man to search
the notary's books, and the contract of marriage with his wife, or any other waie that
may discover his estate; and should they
keep him ten yeares, and ten yeares he was
altogether unable to pay a ransome, and
wished that noe man would judge of his
estate by his ellingant clothes."

The grievances of the French General do
not seem to be of a very substantial character.
He seems to have been treated like a gentleman; and although his host may have been
rather brutal about the laundress, no doubt
he was quite right in keeping up the respecta-
bility of his house. The other French prisoners all bore willing testimony to the kind

G

treatment they had received. Nicholas Blundell, of Dieppe, in his examination, asserts—
" That he and all the rest of the French taken by Captain Kirke, at Canada, have been well used, and intreated by him in the best manner that he could, and as well as himselfe."

Quebec, and the other forts in Canada and Nova Scotia, had been left under the command of Lewis Kirke,[1] David Kirke having returned to England with his prisoners, several thousand beaver skins, and other stores which he had captured. When he arrived in England, to his great consternation he discovered that his last expedition would prove of little benefit either to himself or his associates. About a month after his departure from England upon his cruize, peace had been declared between France and England, and now as soon as the news of the capture of Quebec reached Paris, the French Government immediately

1 Col. Papers : Vol. VI., No. 23, in which is given a curious letter in French, from Captain Lewis Kirke, to Emery de Caen, written in most complimentary terms.

demanded the restitution of all forts captured by the English since the 24th of April, 1629, and, worse than all, Charles I. had passed his royal word to give them up.[1] It is impossible to divine the motives which influenced the King to make such a promise: it may have been that he was as yet totally ignorant of the value of his conquest, and was only anxious to secure the four hundred thousand crowns, part of Henrietta Maria's dowry, which the French King threatened to withhold unless the American forts were restored. But he could not have ignored the fact that he was inflicting a most grievous injury upon the Canada merchants, who, at a cost of £60,000, had fitted out a fleet, and that their only chance of remuneration was in keeping the settlements which they had conquered.

---

1 French Correspondence. Memorial of the French Ambassador to King Charles. Col. Papers : Vol. V., No. 51. See also letters of Sir Isaac Wake, on March 22, April 1, 1632, in French Correspondence, where a great deal of correspondence between the English Ambassador in France and the Home Government, concerning Canada, will be found.

It is impossible, too, to deprecate too strongly this determination of the King's to surrender colonies, which, more than a century afterwards, England had again to conquer at an immense expense both of money and bloodshed. However, Charles had given his word that everything was to be restored to its original state; and those that know his firmness, may I say obstinacy, of disposition, will have little doubt that he kept his word. Memorial after memorial was sent in by the French ambassador to King Charles I., for restitution of all places taken by the English in Canada since the treaty of Susa, particularly the fortress and settlement of Quebec, possessed by Captain Kirke, and those of Cape Breton and Port Royal, possessed by Sir William Alexander: secondly, for permission to seize furs and other merchandize brought in two vessels by the Kirkes from Canada. King Charles hastens to fulfill all their wishes. A commission is issued to Sir Humfrey May, Sir John Coke, Sir Julius

Cæsar, and Sir Henry Marten, "to discover what goods, merchantdise and other things have been taken by Captain David Kirke from the French, from the fort of Quebec, the College of Jesuits, and a French vessel.[1] Not content with this, a warrant is issued to search the warehouse of the Canada merchants, and deliver all the beaver skins to M. de Caen.[2] In vain Kirke petitions the King, telling him that out of the seven thousand skins which he brought home only thirteen hundred were taken from Quebec, the rest were obtained by trading with the Indians; that the French had consumed in victuals much more than the value of thirteen hundred skins, in proof of which he sent in an account of debts between himself and De Caen. But all to no purpose; Kirke and De Caen were summoned before the Lord Mayor, and Kirke was ordered to deliver up the key of the warehouse where the skins were kept. This he refuses

1 March 5th, 1630.

2 Order of Privy Council, April 9th, 1630.

to do; a warrant is then issued to the Lord Mayor[1] and Sheriffs, authorizing them to break down the door, which they do, and seize the skins; Kirke and his party, with the assistance of one Fitz, a merchant, again break open the door and carry off the skins. A warrant is issued for the apprehension of Fitz, who is brought before the Star Chamber, for "great contempt and affront of all authority and justice," and he is sentenced to remain in the Fleet, and not to be suffered to go abroad. This brings Fitz and his friends to their senses, so the beaver skins are restored and Fitz is set at liberty.[2]

But though the beaver skins were lost, Captain Kirke determined to make one more effort to save Quebec. After capturing that place, he had been so struck by the settlement—its impregnable heights, excellent harbours, and central position—that he was loth

1 James Campbell was Lord Mayor this year. Col. Papers: Vol. V., No. 81.

2 Order of the Privy Council, June 16, 1630. Colonial Correspondence, 1630. Appendix 2.

to hand it over to the enemy. He knew that, well victualled and supplied with ammunition, the fortress would withstand the attack of an army, so he presented an humble petition to the King, pointing out the strength of the place, its beauty, the cost to himself and his fellow-adventurers in acquiring it, and how he would guarantee to hold it against an army of Frenchmen; to quote his own manly words, "The above fort (Quebec) is so well situated that they are able to withstand 10,000 men, and will not care for them; for in winter they cannot stay in the country, soe that whosoever goes to besiege them cannot stay above three months, all in which time the musketts[1] will soe tormente them that noe man is able to be abroad in centry or trenches daye or night without losinge their sights at least eight dayes. Soe that if it please your Majesty to keepe it, wee doe not care what French or any other can doe, though she have a hundred sayle of ships and 10,000 men as above sayd."[2]

1 Mosquitoes.   2 Col. Papers : Vol. VI., No. 38.

But all was of no avail; the King had given his word, and no argument on the part of David Kirke could shake his determination. However, the losses of the Canada merchants were so great and palpable, that Charles could not refuse to compensate them to some extent. Commissioners were appointed on behalf of the Canada Company and M. de Caen and his associates: Sir Isaac Wake, the English ambassador in Paris, and M. Burlamachi were appointed the English agents, and M. de Caen appeared for himself and Company. After considerable correspondence it was agreed that the French Government should pay to Captain Kirke £20,000, and that the forts in Canada should be delivered to De Caen whole and entire, with supplies and ammunition. Kirke was thoroughly disgusted with the treaty which Sir Isaac Wake had concluded. He wrote an indignant letter to Wake, denouncing the whole business, denying that he had followed the instructions which the Company had sent him, complaining of the unreasonable demands of De Caen, the restitution of the "Helen" and her goods, and having to pay for beaver skins which they had never received. He concludes by saying, "I conceive the carriage of the business to have been very unequal, and it is plain that the depositions of the French are fully approved, and the English wholly rejected."[1] To conclude this business, it may as well be stated that the French Government repudiated their engagement, and never paid the Kirkes a penny of the £20,000.

On the 12th of June, 1632, the King issued a commission to Sir William Alexander, Robert Charlton, and William Berkeley, appointing them Commissioners for Canada, to receive the forts from Captain Lewis Kirke, Governor thereof, and to deliver them up to the French. "The King having consented to the restitution of the fort and habitation of Quebec, as taken by force of arms since the

[1] April 24, 1632. Col. Papers : Vol. VI., No. 53. Signed by David Kirke, "for my mother, Elizabeth Kirke."

peace, and preferring, notwithstanding the commission given by him during the war, the accomplishment of his own royal word, the Commissioners are commanded—upon the first convenience of sending into those ports, and of means for the people to return—to order all the King's subjects, as well soldiers in garrison as inhabitants and planters, to give up possession to those appointed by the French King, in the same state as at the time of taking. Any person showing himself cross or refractory will receive the King's highest displeasure and indignation, and the punishment due to offenders of so high a nature." [1]

The surrender was at length completed with consequences in after years troublous and expensive to England. From this time, to its final conquest in 1759 by General Wolfe, Canada was the seat of incessant hostilities between the English and French. It is impossible to say what the course of affairs

[1] Col. Papers: Vol. VI., No. 55. Dated at Greenwich, June 12, 1632.

in America would have been if England had remained in possession of Canada and Nova Scotia; but that such a fact would have exercised an immense influence for restraint, both upon the New England colonies and ultimately upon the progress of the French revolution, there can be little doubt. Whether it would have prevented the revolt of the one, and delayed the outbreak of the other is a doubtful question; but that the surrender to the French by Charles entailed upon this country an immense expenditure of blood and money there can be no doubt. Upon the legal aspect of the question I cannot now enter; suffice it to say that the right of the French to demand the cession of the forts, was at the time considered an open question, and that only the anxiety of Charles I. to maintain the French alliance and to obtain his wife's dowry could have induced the English to entertain the question for a moment.

But though the King had destroyed the fruits of Captain Kirke's expedition, he could

not but admire the determination and courage
which he and his brothers had displayed in
two successive voyages to Nova Scotia and
Canada. So in order to mark his approbation
of their conduct, he made them a grant of
honorary additions to their coat of arms. By
this grant, dated December 1st, 1631, to
Captain David Kirke, Lewis Kirke, Governor
of Canada, Captain Thomas Kirke, and James
Kirke, for valour in vanquishing the French
fleet under the command of M. de Roquemont,
Admiral, bringing him prisoner to England,
and in the following year taking Canada,
and bringing M. Champlain prisoner to England, the coat armour of M. de Roquemont
is granted to Captain David Kirke, and to
his brothers, and their issue for ever, to be
worn in a canton over their paternal coat of
arms.[1] Also, when Charles I. paid his visit
to Scotland, in 1633, he knighted David

1 See Domestic Correspondence, Car. 1. Also Appendix E. Add.
MS., British Museum, 5533 ; and Harleian MS., 1082.

Kirke, at Anderwerk, on the 16th of July in the same year.[1]

Gervase Kirke, the rich London merchant, had died on the 17th day of December, 1629, very soon after his son's return from the conquest of Canada. In the year following his father's death, David Kirke was married to Sarah, daughter of Sir Joseph Andrews, Knt. He obtained a considerable dowry with his wife, which, added to his share of his father's wealth, placed him above any necessity for further exertion and trouble. But he was of too active and energetic a nature; his mind was too full of schemes for travel and plantation, to rest quiet in a state of luxurious ease; his eye was ever turned towards the Far West; that land which had so long filled men's minds with dreams of wealth, dreams never to be fulfilled. But much of that romantic nonsense which the earliest travellers to America evoked, had now evaporated; adventurers no longer expected to find silver houses, supported on

1 See Harleian MS., 6062. Lansdowne MS., 807, f. 62.

golden pillars, or women with their bodies
covered with plates of gold; but they knew
there were boundless plains of richest soil,
grand rivers rushing to the sea, amidst over-
hanging woods of birch and pine; venison to
be had for the shooting, and fish for the
catching; lands rich in beaver, whose skins
were worth their weight in silver, and seas
filled with whales and codfish, affording a
rich harvest to the hardy fisherman.

For a few years, Sir David Kirke was
either unwilling or unable to extend his
schemes of colonization, but it would appear
that they were never abandoned, and that he
was only biding his time, and waiting for an
opportunity favourable to his wishes.   His
early travels had made him familiar with all
the territory now known as British North
America, and his recent exploits in that neighbourhood had made him fully alive to its
commercial and military importance.   Newfoundland, especially, was to him a place of
great interest; he knew the riches of its

fisheries—those shallow banks swarming with
codfish and herrings—its spacious and land-
locked harbours, in any of which the com-
bined navies of the world might float in
safety, and abundantly supplied with fresh
water from streams that poured down from
the rocky shore. He knew well enough that
the wealth of Newfoundland lay in the surrounding seas, and not on the land, although
animals existed there in plenty, which could
afford a rich harvest to the trapper; so
there was no danger of his falling into the
same error as Lord Baltimore, who had gone
to Newfoundland expecting to find a land
flowing with milk and honey, where planting
would succeed as well as in the colonies of
Virginia and Florida. A courtier and Secretary of State, who had spent his days within
the precincts of Whitehall, might be easily
deceived by false reports, knowing little or
nothing of what he had to expect in his new
colony, but such a man as Sir David Kirke
was not so readily taken in. Tossed about

from his earliest youth, amidst the icebergs
and fogs of the Northern Seas, he was not
likely to be mistaken in his estimate of the
climate and capabilities of the countries which
they surrounded; in fact, I think it may be
asserted, that if there was one man in England at this period, who knew more than any
other about these distant latitudes, he was
that man. During his enforced idleness in
England, Sir David watched with great interest the progress of Lord Baltimore's attempt
to found a colony at Ferryland. He must
from the first have been persuaded that the
attempt must fail; the wrong man was in the
wrong place, and nothing but disappointment
and distress could follow upon ignorance and
gullibility. He saw poor Lord Baltimore
die at his post, worn out by incessant toil
in a severe climate, aggravated by the chagrin
of repeated failures; yet he was not frightened
from his purpose. For some years he remained in England, trying to obtain from the
French, part, at least, of the money they had

agreed to pay him; but, finding all his efforts of no avail, he determined to obtain a grant of part of Newfoundland from the King, and try whether he could not succeed where so many before him had failed.

CHAPTER III.

WHO was the first discoverer of Newfoundland, is a question which has excited a great deal of discussion, and no little difference of opinion amongst the various writers upon this subject.   Though Columbus and Cabot may one or other of them claim the discovery of the mainland of America,   Mr. Laing[1] and

1 Chronicle of the Kings of Norway :. Vol I., p. 154.   "The discovery of America, or Vinland, in the 11th century, by the same race

other writers seem fully persuaded that the island of Newfoundland was discovered about the year A.D. 1000, by an Icelander. The Saga, which gives an account of this discovery, was undoubtedly written about the year 1387, being found verbatim in the Codex Flatoyensis.[1] It was also committed to writing in Iceland, a century nearly before Columbus visited that country to obtain the nautical information on which he proceeded on his voyage of discovery. The account consists of eight chapters, and is inserted in the Saga of Olaf Tryggvesson. The following

of enduring, enterprising seamen, is not less satisfactorily established by documentary evidence than the discovery and colonization of Greenland; but it rests exclusively upon documentary evidence, which cannot, as in the case of Greenland, be substantiated by anything to be discovered in America."

1 The Flateyar Anual, or Codex Flatoiensis, by far the most important of Icelandic MSS., takes its name from the island Flatö, in Bredefiord, in Iceland, where it had been long preserved, and where Bishop Swendson, of Skalholt, purchased it, about 1650, from the owner, Jonas Torfeson, for King Frederic III., giving in exchange for it the perpetual exemption from land tax of a small estate of the owner. The MS. is a large folio, beautifully written on parchment. The Codex Flatoiensis is not an original work of one author, but a collection of Sagas, transcribed from older MSS., and arranged so far chronologically that the accounts are placed under the reign in which the events they tell of happened.

is an epitome of the whole:—Eric the Red, was a great man who lived in Greenland; he had three sons, Leif, Thorwald, and Thorstein, and his daughter was called Freydis. She was married to a man named Thorwald. She was a haughty, proud woman, and he was a mean man, much given to making money. The people in Greenland were heathen at this time. Biorne, an Icelander, sailed from Iceland, intending to join his father in Greenland, but he lost his way, and was carried he knew not whither. He passed through great fogs, driven by the north wind, and at length, after many days, he made the land. They thought it could not be Greenland, but as they sailed past they saw the land was without mountains, was covered with wood, and had small hills inland. Biorne afterwards passed two other countries, but when his men wished him to land, he said, "This land is not what we want," and sailed on his way, till at length he reached Greenland in safety.

Lief, son of Eric, having heard of Biorne's adventure, determined to visit this land newly found, so he mans a ship, and tries to persuade Eric, his father, to take command, but the old man refuses, so Lief sails without him. He first came to the land which Biorne had last seen, and sailing up to it, cast anchor, and went on shore. No grass was to be seen, and there were large snowy mountains up the country. And Lief said, "It shall not be said of us, as it was of Biorne, that we did not come upon the land, for I will give the country a name, and call it Helloland," which means a land of naked rocks. They then went to sea again, and found another land, which was covered with wood. Then Lief said, "We will give this land a name according to its kind, and call it Markland." They then went to sea again, and found an island. They liked this country so well that they determined to winter there; there was plenty of salmon, and plenty of fodder for cattle, as there was no frost in winter. Days and

nights were more equal than in Greenland or
Iceland. Lief divided his men into two parties, one of which used to explore the interior
of the country. In their explorations they
discovered great quantities of grapes and self-
sown wheat in the fields, and a tree that is
called Massur. Towards the spring, they
sailed away, and Lief called the land Winland,
because of the grapes. Lief arrived in safety
at Greenland, where he became a person of
great consequence, and was called Lief the
Lucky.

This expedition to Winland was much talked
of; so Thorwald, Lief's brother, thought that
he should like to visit the country. So he
set sail in his brother's boat, and arrived in
safety at the booths which Lief had erected
on the new country; where he remained
quietly during the winter. In the spring,
they explored the country to the south, and
found it beautiful and well wooded. They
also sailed to the north, where they met with
bad weather, and were driven on shore. Here

they found three skin boats, and underneath them nine men, eight of whom they killed, but the other escaped. Soon afterwards they were attacked by a great number of the islanders; so they retreated to their ships, and Thorwald said, "We shall put up our war-screens along the gunwales, and defend ourselves as well as we can, but not use our weapons much against them." Which they did. The Skrœlingers shot at them with arrows for some time, then fled. So, said Thorwald, "Are any wounded?" and they replied, "Nobody." Then, said he, "I am wounded with an arrow, and it will be my death wound. You must bury me in this place." So they buried him and returned to Greenland.

Not long afterwards, Thorstein and his wife, Gudrid, sailed to Winland, and there Thorstein died; and his wife returned to Greenland, where she married Thorfinne Karlsefne. After their marriage, Thorfinne and his wife got together a crew of sixty

men and five women, and set sail for Winland, intending to settle there; and for that
purpose they took some cattle with them.
They arrived at Lief's booths, and there established themselves. They soon began a
profitable trade with the natives, who exchanged furs for knives and other wares. The
natives took a great fancy to the strangers'
weapons and wished to buy some, but this
Thorfinne had strictly forbidden. One of
them, however, managed to steal a battle-axe,
and, wishing to test its efficiency, he split open
· the head of one of his countrymen, and killed
him on the spot. This so alarmed his companions, that they took the weapon from him
and threw it into the sea. Thorfinne in a
few years returned to Iceland rich and prosperous. Many other voyages were afterwards
made to Winland; and in 1121, one Eric,
Bishop of Greenland, determined to go to
Winland and convert his countrymen, who
had become heathens.

Such is the account of the Saga, but whether

the land discovered was Newfoundland, is more than doubtful. The description of the country is totally different to what we hear of Newfoundland in later times. A country well wooded, with mountains in the interior, where grapes and corn grew wild, where the winters are very mild, so as to afford abundant fodder all the year round, does not answer at all to the aspect or climate of Newfoundland. But the whole question is so involved in doubt, that it had better be left to the research of antiquaries.

Two brothers, of the name of Xeno, are said to have discovered Newfoundland in 1380; but the account of their adventures is not sufficiently authenticated to be admitted within the bounds of sober history.

But to turn from fable to fact, in the year 1497, John Cabot,[1] with his son, Sebastian,

1 John Stowe's account is as follows :—"This year, A.R., 13 Henry VII., one Sebastian Gabato, a Genoese son born in Bristowe, professing himself to be expert in the knowledge of the circuit of the world and islands of the same (as by his charts, and other reasonable demonstrations, he showed), caused the King to man and victual a ship at Bristowe, to search for an island which he knew to be replenished with rich com-

embarked at Bristol, in the beginning of May, on a voyage of discovery. He took a north-west course, and after considerable difficulties, caused both by the elements and the mutinous spirit of his men, he came in sight of land on the 24th of June, to which he gave the name of Bonavista, a cape still so called on the east coast of Newfoundland. Having landed in the adjoining bay, he saw several natives clothed in skins of animals. He then took possession of the island in the name of the King of England, and called it Baccalaos, which is the native word for cod-fish. On

modities. In the ships, divers merchants of London adventured small stocks; and in the company of this ship sailed also out of Bristowe three or four small ships, fraught with slight and gross wares, as coarse cloths, caps, lace points, and such other. Sir Humfrey Gilbert, Knt., in his book entitled 'On a discoverie of a new passage to Cataia,' writeth thus :—'Sebastian Gabato, by his personall experience and travel, hath sett forth and described this passage in his charts, which are yett to be seen in the Queen's Majestie's Privie Gallery, at White-hall, who was sent to make that discoverie by Kinge Henrie the Seventh, and entered the same fret, affirming that he sailed very far Westward, with a quarter of the North, on the North side of Terra de Librador, the 11th of June, until he came to the Septentaional latitude of 67½°, and finding the sea still open, said that he might and could have gone to Cataia if the enmity of the master and mariners had not been.'"

the Feast of St. John the Baptist, he discovered another smaller island, which he named St. John's. He then proceeded in a south-westerly direction, and explored the coasts, taking possession, as he proceeded, for the Crown of England, until finding himself short of provisions he returned to England. John Cabot brought home no treasures of gold and silver, but he gave such an account of the immense quantities of fish on the coasts of Newfoundland, that the English merchants were roused to activity by the desire to reap some benefit from such a rich harvest.

The other European nations were not long behind England in these latitudes. Gaspar de Corte Real, a Portuguese of noble family, set sail from Lisbon in the year 1501, and after a long voyage, arrived at Newfoundland, in a wide and deep bay, which he called Conception Bay, a name which it still bears. He explored the whole east coast of that island, and then proceeded to the mouth of the great river of Canada, the St. Lawrence.

After this he discovered a land which he called
Terre Verte, or Greenland. He returned to
Portugal; and in a second voyage to that
part of the world, he is supposed to have
been murdered by the Esquimaux.[1]

In the year 1502, Hugh Elliot and Thomas
Ashenhurst, merchants of Bristol, obtained
from Henry VII. letters patent for the establishment of a colony in Newfoundland, but
we have no information whether they ever
set on foot any voyages thither.

According to Bergeron, a French historian,
the fishermen of Normandy and Brittany
visited the great fishing banks near Cape
Breton, in the year 1504, to which place
they gave its name. Two voyages, one by
Jean Denis to Newfoundland in 1506, and
another (1508) by Thomas Hubert, are mentioned by Doctor Forster.

In the year 1527, Robert Thorne, a merchant of Bristol, first conceived the fatal idea
of a north-west passage to India, that idea

1 History of Newfoundland, by Anspach, p. 38.

which has cost the lives of so many gallant
men, only when discovered to be found use-
less. He presented a memorial to Henry
VIII. on this subject, and though involved
in other affairs, the King ordered two ships
to be manned and filled with all necessaries
for a voyage. In these ships Thorne sailed
on the 20th of May. On their arrival at
Newfoundland, one of the ships was lost on
the coast of Labrador. The other ship, called
the "Dominus Vobiscum," sailed along the east
coast of Newfoundland, towards Cape Breton
and Nova Scotia, frequently lying to and
sending parties on shore to explore the country.
The adventurers returned home in the beginning of October, disappointed in their
hopes of discovering a north-west passage.

France, taken up with her designs upon
Naples and Sicily, had up to this time con-
tributed nothing in the field of maritime discovery. Filled with high and romantic no-
tions of chivalry, the French king and nobles
affected to despise every thing connected

with trade and commerce. However, in the
year 1534, Francis I. sent a fleet from St.
Malo, under the command of Francis Cartier,
which arrived at Newfoundland on the 10th
of May. As Cartier's voyage principally con-
cerns Canada, I have given an account of it
in an earlier part of this work, so I shall
not refer to it further in this place.

In the meanwhile, England was not inat-
tentive to her interests in North America. A
London merchant, named Hoare, proposed a
plan for making a settlement in Newfoundland,
and was joined by many young men of position, who were anxious to share in the risks
of the expedition. In Hakluyt's account of
this voyage, Mr. Hoare is described as a tall
and elegant man, of insinuating manners,
clever mind, and abundant means. His associates were Mr. Tuck, a gentleman of Kent;
Tuckfield Thomas Butts, son of Sir William
Butts, of Norfolk; Messrs. Hardie, Biron,
Carter, Wright, Rastall, Ridley, Weekes, and
several others, in all thirty persons, of good

birth and property, who all embarked with Hoare in his ship, called the "Trinity," of 140 tons burden. In another ship, the "Minion," went Messrs. Armigale Wade, (afterwards Clerk of the Council to Henry VIII. and Edward VI.); Oliver Daubeny, a merchant of London; Joy, afterwards gentleman of the Chapel Royal; and several others.

On the 30th of April, 1536, they sailed from Gravesend, and remained at sea for two months without sight of land, till they made Cape Breton. They next arrived at Penguin Island, off the south coast of Newfoundland, where they found an immense quantity of sea-birds. These they found were very good eating when skinned and dressed. Black and white bears were also numerous, and formed a welcome addition to their stock of provisions.

From this small island they proceeded to Newfoundland, where they saw several of the natives, who, however, fled at their approach. Mr. Hoare and his friends remained there till their provisions became short, and being afraid

to go to sea without victuals, they were reduced to feed upon herbs, roots, and shellfish,
and were in the greatest distress; nay, it is
even asserted they fed upon the flesh of one
of their dead companions.[1]

An opportunity of escape at length presented
itself. A French ship laden with provisions
entered the harbour, which Hoare and his
associates made themselves masters of, and
having turned out the French, they placed
them in their own ship, which they had
abandoned, and hastened away in the French
ship. It must be told, however, that they
left the poor Frenchmen plenty of food. The
adventurers arrived at St. Ives, in Cornwall,
at the end of October, so much altered in

---

1 Hakluyt's words are—"And it fortuned that one of the Company
or Crewe of one of the vessels, driven with hunger to seek abroad for
relief, found in the fields the savour of broiled flesh, and fell out with
one for that he would suffer him and his fellows to starve, enjoying
plenty as he thought. And this matter growing to cruel speeches, he
that had the broiled meat burst out into these words, 'If thou wouldst
needs know, the broiled meat that I had was a piece of such a man's
buttock.' The report of this brought to the ship, the captain found
what became of those that were missing, and was persuaded that some
of them were neither devoured by wild beasts nor yet destroyed by
savages."

appearance by their sufferings, that Sir William
Butts and his lady are said to have been unable for some time to recognize their son.

Despite these drawbacks, the English trade
in Newfoundland increased every year. Sailing from the English ports in the spring, their
ships returned in the autumn with their whole
freight of fish salted and dried on the Island.
The trade in a few years became of so much
importance, that in the year 1549, an Act
was passed for the better encouragement of
the fisheries in Iceland and Newfoundland.
These fisheries proved to be of such great value
that many attempts were made to colonize the
Island; but the first attempt which obtained
any amount of success was that of Sir Humphrey Gilbert, in the year 1583. This distinguished man was descended from an old
family in the county of Devon: he was
remarkable in a remarkable age for his knowledge both of the theory and practice of war,
cosmography and navigation, in addition to
an enterprising spirit, and cool intrepidity.

I

Queen Elizabeth, with whom he was a great
favourite,·by letters patent, dated 11th of June,
1578, invested him with full powers to discover, settle, and regulate any remote countries
not in the actual possession of any Christian
princes.[1]

Sir Humphrey received assurances of support from many distinguished men, who declared their intention of accompanying him
on his voyage. When the vessels were ready
for sea, a panic fell upon many of those who
refused to go, but Sir Humphrey still determined to proceed with a few friends who
still remained staunch. He sailed immediately
in the summer of 1578 for Newfoundland,
where he made a short stay, and came back
to England, having narrowly escaped, with
the loss of one vessel, from a squadron of

---

1 In Domestic Correspondence, Eliz., Vol. xcv., No. 63, Cal., p. 475,
will be found a petition to the Queen, dated 22nd March, 1574, to
allow of an enterprise for discovery of sundry rich and unknown lands
"fatally reserved for England and for the honour of your Majestie,"
which is endorsed by Sir Humphrey Gilbert, Sir George Peckham, Mr.
Carlile, and Sir Richard Greenvile, and others, "voiagers."

Spanish men-of-war, by which he had been intercepted.

Sir Humphrey Gilbert, not at all discouraged by his disappointment in the first enterprise, sold his estate, which produced a considerable sum, and, liberally assisted by Sir George Peckham, and other friends, fitted out a small fleet of five ships. This fleet sailed from Cawsand Bay, near Plymouth, on the 11th June, 1583, and consisted of the "Delight," 120 tons, of which Sir H. Gilbert took the command, and appointed William Winter his captain; the "Raleigh," 200 tons, fitted out and commanded by Sir Walter Raleigh; the "Golden Hind," of 40 tons, Edward Hayes, master and captain; the "Swallow," 40 tons, Maurice Brown, captain; and the "Squirrel," of 10 tons, William Andrews, captain. On the 13th, Sir Walter Raleigh was obliged to put back, on account of a distemper which had seized upon the captain and crew. On the 30th of July, they first discovered land, but imperfectly, on account of a dense fog. They next arrived at Penguin Island, where they took in a good stock of birds. After this they entered Conception Bay, where they found the "Swallow," which had been lost in the fog. Then proceeding to the south, they made the Bay of St. John's, where they found the "Squirrel," which had been refused admittance into that harbour by vessels of different nations. Sir Humphrey prepared to force an entrance into the harbour, but before doing so he sent word to the people within the harbour that he came in Queen Elizabeth's name, to take formal possession of the place, and that if he met with any resistance, he should punish the offenders, as he had the will and the power to do. Upon receiving this assurance, the people sent him word that their intentions were peaceable, and that they had only waited to learn the object of his expedition; and that they should be very glad to supply the necessities of his fleet. The ships then entered the harbour, and the next morning Sir Humphrey and his friends

were conducted on shore by the owners of
the English vessels. On the 5th of August
he caused a tent to be erected on the shore,
and summoning all the English and foreign
merchants to attend, he caused his commission under the great seal of England to be
opened and read, and translated to those
foreigners who did not understand English.
He then informed the assembly that, under
the Royal authority, he stood possessed of
St. John's and all the adjacent land within
the circumference of 200 leagues; and that
thenceforward the witnesses of this transaction
must consider these territories as belonging
to the Sovereign of England, and acknowledge
that he, the General of Queen Elizabeth, was
empowered by Royal license to possess and
enjoy them, and likewise to enact laws for
the government thereof. The customary
ceremony of delivering a rod and turf to the
new proprietor, was then performed in the
presence of the assembly.

Sir Humphrey then, by virtue of his

authority, proceeded to issue certain regula-
tions for the religious and civil government
of the island, to which all the people promised obedience. The meeting was then dissolved ;· and on the same spot the General
erected a wooden pillar, to which he attached
the arms of England, engraved on lead. He
then granted several parcels of land to be
held of him, his heirs and assigns, for ever,
on the payment of certain rent and services;
and having done this, he issued orders for
the collection of a tax upon the vessels in the
harbour, to be paid in provisions.

Whilst some of the English were collecting
provisions, and performing other duties, Sir
Humphrey sent several exploring parties into
different parts of the country. The result of
their observations was that there were but
few men on the southern part of the island,
but in the north they met with some of the
natives, who showed no fear, and approached
them at once, without hesitation. The climate
is reported as being very hot in summer and

extremely cold in winter. The sea abounded
with codfish; they had also observed turbot,
lobsters, and herrings; whales were found in
great numbers, and in the bays and rivers
there were salmon and trout in great abundance. The whole country was covered with
wood; game was very plentiful, and they
could easily procure hides and furs of all
kinds. They also stated that the soil was
very fertile, and that they had discovered
mines of iron, lead, copper, and silver. One
Daniel, a native of Saxony, and an expert
miner, brought a piece of ore to Sir Humphrey, which he positively asserted to contain
a considerable quantity of silver. The credulous General was enchanted with this piece of
ore, carried it on board, and enjoined the
strictest secrecy, for fear that the French and
Portuguese should hear of the precious discovery.[1]

---

1 Sir Humphrey was so delighted with this discovery, that he boasted
to his friends that he could obtain from Queen Elizabeth a loan of
£10,000 on the credit of the mine.

A mutiny broke out about this time amongst the English, to prevent the continuation of the voyage. But though the conspiracy was discovered, yet a great number of the sailors deserted, and seizing a ship laden with fish, compelled her crew to go ashore, and immediately set sail for England. Of the rest, some fell ill and died, and others were allowed to return to England in the Swallow, under Captain Winter.

"The three remaining vessels being completely fitted for the intended voyage, the General hoisted his flag on board the Squirrel, a light and expeditious sailer, and the best constructed for the purpose of entering creeks and small harbours. He gave the command of the Delight to Captain Maurice Brown, and the Golden Hind to Captain Edward Hayes. On the 20th of August, they sailed from the harbour of St. John's, which they found by observation to be in 47 degrees, 40 minutes, N. latitude. In the following night they made Cape Race, distant 25 leagues,

and from thence nearly 87 leagues towards
Cape Breton.   On the 27th, in the latitude
of 45 degrees, Sir Humphrey gave orders to
sound, and at the depth of 30 fathoms, they
found white sand; in the succeeding afternoon the wind veered to the S., when, in
opposition to the advice of William Cox,
master of the Golden Hind, the ships bore
in, with the land during the whole night at
W.N.W.   The next day it blew a violent
storm at S. by E.; the rain descended in
torrents, and the fogs were so extremely
thick, that no object could be distinguished
at a cable's length.   Towards daybreak on
the 29th, they were alarmed by the appearance of surrounding sands and shoals, and at
every third or fourth ship's length, observed
the water lessening in its depth.   A signal
was thrown out for the Delight to stand off
to sea, but at that very instant she struck,
and soon after her stern and quarters were
dashed to pieces.   The Squirrel and the
Golden Hind, immediately casting about

E.S.E., and bearing to the S., with great
difficulty got clear of the shoal, and
regained the open sea.   In the Delight
perished Captain Maurice Brown, and about
100 of his associates, who, with a resolution
that bordered upon madness, refused to set
what they thought a bad example, by deserting the ship, although they must have been
convinced that it was impossible to save her.
Fourteen of her crew leaped into a small
pinnace, and remained a short time alongside
their ship, in the hope of being joined by
their captain, but in vain.   Having, at last
prevailed upon Richard Clarke, the master,
and one of his companions, to join them,
they cut the rope and ventured out to sea,
furnished only with a single oar, and destitute
of fresh water and provisions.   As the pinnace appeared to be much overladen, Edward
Headley proposed the casting of lots, so that
four of them might be thrown overboard.
Clarke, whom it had been unanimously agreed
to except from this measure, availing himself

of their affectionate regard for him, succeeded in persuading them to bear their present lot with Christian fortitude.

The pinnace was driven before the wind during six days and nights, while these men were reduced to feed upon some weeds which they picked up upon the surface of the sea. Sinking under the sufferings of thirst, hunger, intense cold, and constant fatigue, Headley and another man expired on the fifth day; and on the seventh, the remaining fourteen were fortunately driven towards the coast of Newfoundland, where they obtained a passage in a French vessel, and at last arrived safely in England." [1]

The melancholy fate of the Delight was most distressing to Sir Humphrey, not only for the loss of a valuable ship, and tried and sincere friends, but also for the loss of the Saxon miner and his silver ore, upon the evidence of which he had expected to obtain a loan from Queen Elizabeth. The loss of

1 History of Newfoundland, p. 70.

the Delight frightened the remaining ships'
companies, so the General determined to return to England, and resisted all the attempts
of the captain of the Golden Hind to dissuade
him from his design. " Be content," said
he, " we have seen enough; take no thought
of the expenses which we have incurred. If
the Almighty should permit us to reach England in safety, I will set you out royally
in the course of the next spring; therefore
I pray you, let us no longer strive here,
where we fight against the elements."

On the 1st September the vessels changed
their course for England, and on the 2nd
passed Cape Race. Some days afterwards,
Sir Humphrey came on board the Golden
Hind, to have a wound in his foot dressed,
received by treading on a nail. Captain
Hayes entreated him to remain in his ship,
as the Squirrel was tossing in the waves,
and seemed in danger of being swallowed up
every moment. He, however, refused, saying
that no inducement should cause him to

abandon his brave comrades. Then, to quote
from Captain Hayes, "When off the Azores,
the storms came on worse, with terrible seas,
breaking short and pyramid wise," and on
the 9th of September, the Squirrel having
nearly gone down, but recovering herself,
"the General, sitting abaft, with a book in
his hand, cried out to us in the Hind, as
oft as we did approach within hearing, 'we
are as near heaven by sea as by land,'
reiterating the same speech, well beseeming
a soldier resolute in Jesus Christ, as I can
testify he was. The same Monday, about
twelve of the clock, or not long after, the
frigate being ahead of us in the Golden Hind,
suddenly her lights were out; and withal
our watch cried, the General was cast away,
which was true; for in that moment the
frigate was devoured and swallowed up by
the sea." So perished Sir Humphrey Gilbert,
one of the noblest and best of men in an age
of great men. The Golden Hind arrived
safely at Falmouth on the 22nd September.

Of the fate of the Swallow nothing was ever heard.

Richard Strange, of Apshan, was the next to make a voyage to the island. He was the first who went there expressly for the seal fishery, as most of the ships confined their attention to codfish and whales. Strange sailed from Falmouth on the 1st June, 1593, with two ships, viz., the "Marigold," of 70 tons, and another ship, having on board several butchers and coopers. They sailed for the Island of Ramea, on the back of Newfoundland to the S.W. This island abounded in walrus, a kind of large seal, with two large tusks of ivory, which, together with their skins and oil, were considered valuable articles of commerce. The ships had separated during the voyage; the smaller one arrived in safety at the Island of Ramea. On the 11th of July, the Marigold made Cape St. Francis at the entrance of Conception Bay; then having doubled Cape Race, sailed towards the Bay of St. Peter's; but as they

were at a loss which way to steer, they lost
their way, and fell upon Cape Breton, where
they went on shore, and saw several of the
natives. They then went away to the S.W.,
and at the distance of 60 leagues from the
Cape, they saw immense numbers of seals,
and some whales of enormous size. After
hovering about the Coast of Nova Scotia for
eleven weeks, they returned home to England
by the Azores.

The year following, Captain Richard Jones
sailed from Bristol for the Gulf of St. Lawrence, with a barque of 35 tons. On the 19th
May he reached Cape Spear, on the Coast of
Newfoundland, and proceeded to the Island
of St. Peter, where, laying his vessel upon
the lee, the crew, in less than two hours,
caught 300 codfish, which served for provisions. They returned to Bristol on the 24th
September.

A great number of ships of all the European
nations were at this time collected on the
banks of Newfoundland. Little or no autho-

rity was exercised over them, and divers acts
of piracy were committed with impunity.
There is a curious account of a piracy committed by three French ships, off Newfoundland, in the year 1596, upon one Richard
Clarke. The principal French ship was commanded by Michael de Sanci, and the next
ship by Martin de Sanci. Having been used
with kind entertainment and invited to break-
fast (September 25), in requital Clarke invited
the Frenchmen on board his ship to dinner
the next day; the Captain of the Admiral
framed an excuse, and sent the same afternoon
for Clarke to visit him in his sickness, and
upon a sudden the Frenchmen crying Rend
vous! Rend vous! Clarke and his men were
taken and kept prisoners nine days. After
pillaging their ship, it was delivered up to
them altogether unfurnished.[1]

Hearing of such acts as these, it was not
to be wondered at that Charles Leigh and
Abraham van Herwick, two London mer-

1 Col. Papers : Vol. I., No. 8.

chants, who sailed to Newfoundland in the
next year, should have gone well armed and
prepared to defend their cargo. These ships
were the "Hopewell," of 120 tons, and the
"Chancewell," of 70 tons. They left Gravesend on the 8th of April, 1597, and on the
18th of May reached the fishing banks, and
on the 20th they came to Conception Bay.
The "Hopewell," leaving the bay, after having caught a large quantity of codfish, went
to the Isle of Ramea in search of seals. Here
she fell in with four foreign ships, with all of
which she engaged at once, but, overpowered
by numbers, she was obliged to retreat, having
lost her pinnace, together with a cable and
anchor. The "Chancewell" was unfortunately
lost upon Cape Breton; but eight of the
mariners, who had put to sea in a small boat,
were picked up by the "Hopewell." On the
25th of July, the "Hopewell," being in the
harbour of St. Mary, attacked a ship belonging
to Bellisle, of 200 tons and forty men, and
took her after a long and severe action. Mr.

K

Leigh having despatched the " Hopewell " to
the Azores, proceeded in his prize on his return to England, and arrived at Gravesend
in the beginning of September, with a valuable
cargo of fish and oil.

At the beginning of the 17th century, the
Island of Newfoundland occupied a considerable share of public attention. In the year
1609, one, John Guy,[1] an alderman, of Bristol,
published a treatise on the advantages which
would result to England from the establishment of a colony in that Island; this treatise
produced such an effect that a Company was

1 In the Bristol MS. Calendar there is the following account of these
expeditions : " Mr. John Whitson and Mr. Robert Aldworth, and others,
set forth a ship for the discovery of the N.W. passage, under the command of Martin Prynne, being then but twenty-three years of age, who
after proved a very good seaman in the East India voyages. He is
buried in St. Stephen's, on the north side of the chancel. In the year
1609, Mr. John Guy, merchant, one of the Council of Bristol, intending a plantation in Newfoundland, procured a licence and charter from
the King for the same, having some rich merchants of London, and
many of this city did put in their money with them. And so Mr. Guy
and some other young merchants went over to make trial whether the
land could bear corn. They also carried cattle and swine over with them
to increase the land." And again, we read that " In the year 1611
Mr. John Guy, merchant, went to Newfoundland, victualled for a plantation of forty men for the whole year."

immediately formed to carry out the idea, consisting of the Earl of Northampton, Sir Francis Bacon, Sir Lawrence Tanfield, and others. To this Company, King James I., by letters patent dated May 2, 1610, made a grant of all Newfoundland, from 46 to 52 degrees of N. latitude, together with the seas and islands lying within ten leagues of the coast, reserving to all manner of persons of what nation soever, as well as the English, the right of trade and fishing in the parts aforesaid. Under this patent a colony was sent to the island under the direction of Mr. John Guy, who was appointed Governor of the same. After a voyage of twenty days, Guy arrived and landed near Conception Harbour, in a cove now called Mosquito. Here huts were immediately constructed, and Guy behaved with such prudence and kindness to the natives that he quickly gained their confidence, and was permitted to carry on his measures without hindrance. He also established a means of trading with the Indians to

their mutual satisfaction. In an account of
Newfoundland, which Sir David Kirke sent
to the English merchants about twenty years
later,[1] he gives some curious information relating to Guy's transactions with the Indians.
He says (in answer to an objection that there
was no trade with the natives)—"First, say
you, if there be a trade there must be some-
body supposed with whom to trade, and there
be noe natives upon the island. How noe
natives upon the island of Newfoundland?
Have you left your eyesight in the Fogges
againe, and so blinded do you know at whom
you strike? How comes it to pass, I pray
you, that His Majesty in the beginning of his
patent makes it one of the principal reasons,
for which he granted it, the hope of the conversion of these heathens to the Christian
faith. And that you may be assured there are
such creatures upon Newfoundland, if your
Wisdoms consult but with our poore fisher-

---

1 Col. Papers: Vol. X., No. 38. Endorsed by Archbishop Laud,
"Rec, Feb. 9, 1640."

men, that use to fish in Trinity Bay and more
northerly, they will assure you by their owne
continuall and sad experience, that they have
found too many badd neighbours of the natives almost every fishinge season. And wee
ourselves can assure you that there traded
soe many of them with the French, even this
presint yeare, that if you had been amongst
them you had bene confuted to the purpose
with the hardest bargaine that ever you concluded since you were men of business. The
accident was thus: in the harbour of Les
Ouages, about eighty Indians assaulted a companie of French whilst they were pyleinge
upp their fishinge, and slewe seven of them;
proceedinge a little further killed nine more
in the same manner, and cloathinge sixteen
of their company in the apparell of the slayne
French, they went on the next daye to the
harbour of Petty Masters, and not being sus-
pected by the French that were there by
reason of their habit, they surprised them at
their works and killed twenty-one more. Soe

in two dayes, having barbarously maymed
thirty-seven, they returned home, as is their
manner, in great triumph, with the heads of
the slayne Frenchmen. Thus, it is too apparent to see that there are Indians upon
Newfoundland, by the mischief that they have
done. But that you may be further informed
of what good hath and might have been done
amongst them, take notice of those which
follows: It is very well knowne that in times
past many French and Biscaners have traded
with the natives of the country for furs and
deere skins. For some yeares they continued
their traffique every fishing season, and it
was sometimes intermitted, as quarrells arose
betwixt them. About 20 years since, Alderman Guy, of Bristoll, that had continued with
his family two yeares in Newfoundland, and
amongst his other designs especially aymed
at a trade with the Indians, imployed for that
purpose one Captain Whittington, into the
bottom of Trinity Baye, a place always fre-
quented with the natives, and which the Cap-

taine havinge discovered a companie ashore, commanded his men to land him alone upon a place where there was a fordable river betwixt him and them. After some signes made betwixt them on either side, one of the Indians waded through the water, and when he came near the Captaine he threwe by his bowe and arrowes in token of peace, and upon that they mett and imbrased, but the Indian, feelinge a short faucion, which the Captaine wore under a close coate, he retyred, expressing signes of dislike and feare. And the Captaine, understanding his meaninge, threwe aside his sword alsoe, as the other before had done his bowe and arrowes. Upon that more Indians on the other side the river were called over, and the Captaine caused his servante aboard the boate to bringe ashore provisions of meate and drinke to entertayne them. They did eate and drinke together for the space of three or four houres, and exchanged furs and deere skins for hatchetts and knives, and appointed a meeting the next year by a signe (as is their manner in other parts of America), when the grass should be of such a height, to bring downe all their furrs and skins for traffique with the English. Upon these terms they parted. And it soe fell out the next yeare, that at the tyme appointed for their meetinge in the same place, instead of Captaine Whittington or other agents for the Alderman, there came a fisherman to the place to make a voyage, and seeing a companie of Indians together, not knowing the cause of their coming, let fly his shott from aboard amongst them. And they imagininge these to be the men in all likelyhood which agreed upon the meetinge the yeare before, retyred presently into the woode, and from that day to this have sought all occasion every fishinge season to do all the mischief they can amongst the fishermen. Yet are we not out of hope, but if it be our fortune to light upon them, they may be brought by a fayre intreatie to a trade againe, which we assure ourselves may be very profitable to the lorde and other adventurers, when it shall be our good happ. to make the natives acquainted with our good intentions towards them." [1]

For some reason not known Guy returned to England disappointed in his endeavours to found a colony. Four years afterwards, in 1614, Captain Whitbourne was sent to Newfoundland under a commission from the Admiralty, authorizing him to impannel juries,

[1] Great interest has been manifested at different times in the aborigines of Newfoundland. The first account of them is to be found in Fabyan's Chronicle :—" In the fourteenth year of Henry VII., there were brought unto him three men, taken in Newfound Island by John Cabot. They were clothed in the skins of beasts, and spake such speech that no man could understand them, and in their demeanour were like brute beasts ; whom the King kept a time after, of the which about two years I saw two apparelled after the manner of Englishmen, in Westminster Palace, which at that time I could not discern from Englishmen till I was learned what they were ; but as for speech, I heard none of them utter a word." Instead of following the humane example of Alderman Guy and Sir David Kirke, the different traders and settlers at Newfoundland seem to have treated the poor Bœothics, as they were called, with great brutality, shooting them down like wild beasts. They were also much oppressed by their hereditary enemies, the Micmacs, a tribe of Red Indians, who at some time crossed over to the island from the mainland, and who have at this time several flourishing settlements on the east coast. The Author has been informed by Admiral Sir H. Prescott, G.C.B., who was for many years Governor of Newfoundland, that he went there with the firm conviction that Bœothics were still to be found in the island, but after careful in-vestigation and enquiry, he was persuaded that the race was extinct.

and to enquire upon oath of divers abuses and
disorders committed amongst those who carried
on fishery upon the coast. By virtue of this
commission, Captain Whitbourne held a court
of admiralty immediately after his arrival,
and received the complaints of one hundred
and seventy masters of English ships, shewing
to what an extent of prosperity the English
trade had gained.

The Company of the Plantation in Newfoundland excited the complaints of the fishermen, for depriving them of their rights in
fishery, laying a tax upon their cargoes, and
other exactions. In the year 1618, several
petitions were presented to the Privy Council,
by the fishermen, complaining that the planters
had put sundry of the petitioners from the
chiefest places of fishing; great quantities of
their provisions had been appropriated;
they had been prevented taking birds which
are used as bait; fees had been exacted from
them; and pirates harboured, to their great
prejudice. On 19th October, 1618, the Earl

of Bath incloses a petition of the merchants
of Devon to the Privy Council, concerning
some bad measures offered them in their
fishing in Newfoundland by those of the late
plantation there, which he recommends to
their favourable consideration, and that the
merchants may be secured from further disturbance in the enjoyment of their privileges.[1]
To these complaints the Company replied that
they considered that their chargeable main-
tenance for the colony entitled the inhabitants
to choose their fishing places; know of no
wrongs done to the fishermen; if taking of
birds has been denied, it shall be ordered to
the contrary; utterly disclaim the exaction
of fees; complain that the very great damages
they have received from pirates have almost
overthrown the colony; are desirous to join
with the western men in that business, and for
keeping good order in the country. To this
the fishermen replied that "No privilege had

---

[1] Col. Papers: Vol. I., No. 39, 40. Domestic Correspondence,
James I., Vol. CIII., No. 43, Cal., p. 586.

been given by the charter to planters for fishing before others ; if choice of places is admitted contrary to common usage, the petitioners contend that they ought rather to
have it; desire that the liberties reserved to
them by charter may be confirmed; disclaim
committing any abuses in the country, and
request that the offenders may be punished.
The fishermen, knowing better how to manage
the fishing than the planters can direct, declare that they are altogether unwilling to be
ordered by the planters, or to join with them
as they desire."

The Company seem to have been much
troubled about this time by pirates, who found
a rich harvest amongst the numerous fishing
vessels on the coasts, which had increased to
such numbers, that in 1615 upwards of 250
English vessels were employed in this trade;
and in 1621, more than 300 ships, with 10,000
seamen. The custom of goods imported into
Newfoundlaud produced a yearly revenue of
£10,000. Pirates were not the only pests of

the coasts; some of the disorderly fishermen causing great disturbance, and sometimes actual warfare. To such an extent had this mischief increased, that the Company of Planters petitioned the Crown to make New-foundland a naval station, and send thither a lieutenant, with two or more war ships, to keep order amongst the fishermen and protect them from pirates. At the end of their petition is attached a list of pirates, with the amount of damage which they had inflicted, estimated at £48,000, besides the loss of about 180 pieces of ordnance, and 1,080 fishermen, sailors, carpenters, and gunners, taken by force or otherwise conveyed away.[1]

In the year 1615, Doctor Vaughan purchased from the patentees a tract of land in the southern part of the island, of which he appointed Whitbourne Governor. He established himself at Ferryland, but does not seem to have remained long upon the island.

About this time Newfoundland began to

1 Col. Papers: Vol. I., No. 54.

bear a more settled appearance. Moreover,
fixed war stations were established along the
coasts, and roads were cut through the dense
forests of underwood in the interior to com-
municate from one post to another. St. John's
was selected as the place of rendezvous where
the inhabitants met to ship their skins, or to
exchange them for other stores which had
arrived from England. In the next chapter
we shall enter upon a new phase in the
History of the Island.

CHAPTER IV.

ON the 31st December, 1622, Sir George Calvert obtained from James I. a grant of the whole island of Newfoundland. He had been Secretary to Sir Robert Cecil, and Clerk to the Privy Council, and was knighted in 1617. In the following year he was made

Secretary of State to the King, who settled
£1,000 a year upon him, besides his salary.
In 1624 he became a Roman Catholic, and
so was compelled to resign his post. The
King, however, persuaded him to stay in the
Privy Council, and showed him much favour,
granting him large estates in Ireland, and
at last raised him to the peerage, under the
title of Lord Baltimore. After his conversion,
Sir George seems to have become unsettled
in his mind, and conceiving himself slighted
on account of his religion, determined to
withdraw to some distant spot, where he
might practice his religion without molesta-
tion. So he requested and obtained a grant
of Newfoundland, or rather of the south, or
smaller part of the island, to which district
he gave the name of Avalon.[1] This island

1 It was so called by Lord Baltimore, with the idea that this province was the place in America where Christianity was first introduced,
Avalon being the name of an ancient place in Somersetshire on which
Glastonbury now stands, and which is said to be the place where
Christianity was first preached in Britain. Lord Baltimore's province,
which forms the south-east part of Newfoundland, is a peninsular of
twenty-six marine leagues in length, and from five to twenty in breadth.

seems to have been one of the earliest resorts
of persecuted religious bodies in England,
for about this time, or a little earlier, we
find several settlements of Puritans on its
coasts, who had fled from the rigour of
episcopal government. In the year 1623, Sir
George Calvert sent out a body of men
under Captain Edward Wynne, to prepare
the way for his arrival, and with him sent
£2,500 sterling, as an earnest of what he
intended to do in the colony. Captain Wynne,
on his arrival, established himself at Ferryland, possibly in Doctor Vaughan's abandoned
quarters, where he built the largest house
ever seen on the island; erected granaries and
storehouses, and accommodated his people in
the best manner possible. The following year
he received a reinforcement of colonists, and a
considerable supply of stores and implements,
and soon afterwards the colony was in such

It is separated from the main part of the island by two extensive bays,
the heads of which are divided by a narrow isthmus or beach not ex-
ceeding four miles in width, where it is not unusual to see fishermen
pass from one bay to another, drawing their boats over it with ropes.

L

a flourishing condition, that on the 17th of August he wrote to Sir George Calvert, "We have wheat, barley, oats, and beans, eared and codded; though the late sowing of them, in May or the beginning of June, might occasion the contrary, yet they ripen so fast, that we have all the appearance of an approaching plentiful harvest." In the same strain, he speaks of his garden, his pasture land, and arable cleared since his arrival, and of his numerous herds of cattle.[1] A small workshop and fort were also erected at Ferryland by Captain Wynn, and completed by Mr. Rickson; and so delighted was Sir George (now Lord Baltimore) with the account he received, that he removed to his colony with his family, built a handsome and spacious house, and a strong fort at Ferryland.

Strange as it sounds to our ears, in the

1 These statements must have been gross exaggerations. At the present time, after 200 years of improvement, the best cultivated grounds scarcely bring even oats to perfect maturity. Potatoes and cabbage succeed very well. Currants and gooseberries grow to the greatest perfection; cherries are excellent; and damsons grow in abundance, but seldom ripen.

year 1625, the western ports of England were blockaded by Turkish pirates, and great fears were entertained about the safety of the annual fleet of fishing ships on their return from New-foundland. Letters were sent from the Mayors of Poole and Plymouth to the Privy Council, asserting that unless prompt measures were immediately taken, the Newfoundland fleet of 250 sail would be captured by the pirates. Already 27 ships and 250 persons had been taken by Turkish pirates[1] in ten days.

But the poor fishermen were exposed to worse enemies than the pirates. Admiral de l'Arade, with three French men-of-war, ap-peared off Newfoundland, and reduced the poor fishermen to great extremity; but Lord Baltimore, with two ships, manned at his own expense, drove away the French, and took 60 of them prisoners. Concerning this business, there are extant two very interesting letters of Lord Baltimore's, addressed to Charles I. and the Duke of Buckingham,

1 Domestic Correspondence : Car. I., Vol. V., No. 24, Cal., p. 81.

which give a succinct account of this transaction. To the King he writes:—

" Most gracious and dread Sovereign,—

" In this remote wilde parte of the worlde, where I have planted myselfe, and shall endeavour, by God's assistance, to enlarge your Majestie's dominions, and in whatsoever else to serve your Majestie loyallye and faithfullie with all the powers both of my mynde and bodye, I meete with grate difficulties and incumbrances at the beginninge (as enterprises of this nature commonly have), and cannot bee easilie overcome by such weake hands as myne, without your Majestie's speciall protection: for which cause I must still renew my addresses to your Majestie as your most humble subject and vassall for the continuance of your Princely favour to mee and this worke which I have taken in hand. Your Majestie's subjects fishinge this yeare in the harbours of this land have been much disquieted by a Frenchman of Warre one Monsieur de la Rade, of Deepe, who with three ships and

400 men, well armed and appoynted, came first into a harbour belonging to mee, called Carpebroile, where hee surprised divers of the fishermen, tooke two of their shipps in the harbour, and kept the possession of them till I sent two shipps of mine, with some hundred men, beinge all the fource we coulde make upon the suddayne in this place, where I am planted; uppon the approach of which shipps neare to the harbour's mouth of Cape-broile, one of them being 360 tons, with 24 pieces of ordnance, the ffrench let slip their cables, and made to sea as fast as they could, leaving behind them both the English shipps, whereof they had formerly possession, 67 of their own countrymen on shore, whom I have had since heere with me prisoners. We followed the chase so long as wee saw any possibility of coming upp with them, but they were much better of saile, and wee were forced to give it over. The said De la Rade hath since donne more spoils uppon other of your Majestie's subjects in the N. parts of this

land, as I was given to understand, which
caused me to pursue them a second tyme,
but they weare driven out of the country by
a shipp of London, before myne could gett
thither. Hereuppon, being still vexed with
these men, and both myselfe, in my poore
fisherie heere, and many other of your
Majestie's subjects, much injured this yeare
by them, I directed my ship, in consort with
Captain Fearn's man-of-warre, then in this
country, to seek out some of that nation at
Trepasse, a harbour to the S. where they used
to fish. There they found 6 shipps, 5 of
Bayonne, and one of St. Jean de Luz, whom
they tooke with their lading, being fish and
trayne, and have sent them to England. I
doe humblie beseech your Majestie's gracious
and benigne interpretation of my proceedings,
where the principall end hath been to doe
your Majestie service, and to give me leave
uppon this occasion to be an humble sutor
unto your Majestie, both for myne owne
safetie, and for many thousands of your subjects that use this land, and come hither every

yeare, for the most parte weakely provided
of defences, that by your Majestie's supreame
authority for the preservation of your people,
being seamen and mariners, and their shipps,
from the spoile of the enemye (the loss whereof
much imports your Majestie's service), two
men-of-warre, at leaste, may be appoynted to
guard this coast, and to be heere betymes in
the yeare; the fishermen to contribute to the de-
fraying of the charge, which amongst soe
many will be but a small matter, and easilie
borne. I have humbly intreated my Lord
Duke to recommend and mediate it unto
your Princely wisdome, beseeching your
Majestie to pardon this unmannerly length
wherewith I have presumed to trouble your
patience.

"God Almighty preserve your Majestie
with a long Raygne and much happiness.

"Your Majestie's most loyal subject
and humble servant,

"GEO. BALTIMORE.[1]

"Ferryland, 25 August, 1628."

1 Col. Papers : Vol. IV., No. 56, 57.

In a letter of the same date, addressed to the Duke of Buckingham, Lord Baltimore writes :—

"May it please your Grace,

"I remember that His Majestie once told me that I write as faier a hand to look upon a farre as any man in England, but that when any man came near it they were not able to read a word. Whereuppon I gott a dispensation both from His Majestie and your Grace, to use another man's pen when I write to eyther of you, and I humbly thanke you for it, for writing is a great pain to mee nowe.

"I owe your Grace an account of my actions and proceedings in this plantation, since under your patronage, and by your honourable mediation to His Majestie, I have transplanted myself hither. I came to build, to sett, to sowe, but I am faln to fighting with Frenchmen."

He then goes on to describe his affair with De la Rade, and "La Fleur de la Jennesse de Normandie," in words similar to those in the last letter. He concludes by requesting the Duke to use his influence with the King to induce him to send two men-of-war to New-foundland, to protect the fishery :—

"If your Grace will bee pleased to inter-cede unto His Majestie in that behalf, and that some principall owners of the West country may be conferred withall to that pur-pose, before the next spring, and the contribu-tion imposed heere by His Majestie's authority, I have desired this bearer, Mr. Peasley, some-time a servant of our late Sovereigne, who for company I have had heere this summer, to attend your Grace on my behalf, and I humblye beseech you to vouchsafe me accesse to your person, as there shall be occasion, with favour, and I shall always rest the same, now and for ever,

"Your Grace's most faithfull
and humble servant,
"GEO. BALTIMORE.
"Ferryland, Aug. 25, 1628."

Lord Baltimore's request was granted, and
two prize ships, the "Esperaine" and "S.
Claude," were sent out to Newfoundland,
under the command of Leonard Calvert, his
Lordship's son. Poor Lord Baltimore, queru-
lous and dissatisfied, did not find Newfoundland as pleasant a place as he expected. He
found that Captain Wynne had grossly exag-
gerated about the climate, the summers being
too short to ripen corn, and the island being
almost entirely dependent upon supplies from
abroad. Added to this, he found the free
exercise of his religion no easier in Ferryland
than at Whitehall. The island was filled with
Puritans, who looked with abhorrence at his
papistical observances; and some bold preacher
came and upheld sectarian doctrines under his
very nose at Ferryland. One of these, by
name Erasmus Stourton, burning with religious zeal, thought it his duty to denounce
Lord Baltimore's doings upon his return to
England. He had no sooner landed at Plymouth, than he hastened to present himself

before Nicholas Sherwill, Mayor of Plymouth,
and Thomas Sherwill, merchant, both Justices
of the peace for the borough of Plymouth,
and into their horrified ears he poured his
astounding tale of Lord Baltimore's misdeeds:
how the said Lord arrived in Newfoundland
on the 23rd July, 1627, and brought with
him two seminary priests, one of them called
Langvill, and the other called Anthony Smith;
but Langvill returned to England with the
said Lord, who brought out the same year
another priest, named Hackett, and with him
about 40 papists; and how the said Hackett
and Smith said mass every Sunday, and used
" all the other ceremonies of the Church of
Rome, in the ample manner as 'tis used in
Spain; " and how the child of one William
Poole, a Protestant, was baptised into the
Romish Church, by order of Lord Baltimore,
and contrary to the wish of its father."[1]

No wonder that the worthy brothers Sherwill, amazed at such enormities, sent Stourton

1 Col. Papers: Vol. IV., No. 59.

post haste to the Privy Council, with a copy of his deposition in his pocket.

England and France being now at war (1628), the fishing banks at Newfoundland were infested by French cruisers. Lord Baltimore, hearing that three French men-of-war had appeared off the banks, sent his ship, the "Benediction," together with the "Victory," a ship from London, to drive the French from the island. Not finding the men-of-war, the Benediction and Victory sailed to Trepasse, where they found six French fishing ships. The Benediction, entering the harbour, first gave the French six or seven shots, and then poured in a broadside upon them, which so terrified them, that they abandoned their ships, and made off to the shore. In the meanwhile, the Victory had lowered her boats, and rowing to the French ships, boarded them, and took possession. The two war ships divided these prizes between them, and in a further cruise, were equally fortunate.[1]

1 Col. Papers : Vol. IV., No. 63.

But despite his successes against the French, it is evident that poor Lord Baltimore is heartily sick of Newfoundland. He finds difficulties on every side; his crops failing, his health failing, his men dying, and his religion despised and abhorred. He had heard of Stourton's depositions, and his mind is troubled. In 1629, August 19, he writes to the King, to thank him for the loan of a ship, which had been sent to him. In this letter he complains of the calumny and malice of those who seek to make him appear foul in His Majesty's eyes, and of the slanderous reports raised at Plymouth last winter, by an audacious man, who was banished the colony for his misdeeds. Has met with difficulties in this place no longer to be resisted, and is forced to shift to some warmer climate of the world, where the winters are shorter and less rigorous. He complains of the severity of the weather from September to May; both land and sea frozen the greatest part of the time. His house has been a hospital all the

winter; of 100 persons, 50 sick at one time,
he being one; nine or ten have died. His
strength is much decayed, but his inclination
carries him naturally to proceedings in plantations. In conclusion, he desires a grant of a
precinct of land in Virginia, where he wishes
to remove with 40 persons, with such privileges as King James granted to him in
Newfoundland.[1] In reply to this doleful
epistle, the King wrote him[2] a letter full of
kindness, but at the same time with a dash
of irony. Seeing his plantation in Newfoundland has not answered his expectation, that
he is in pursuit of new countries, and weighing
that men of his condition and breeding are
fitted for other employments than the framing
of new plantations, which commonly have
rugged and laborious beginnings, the King
has thought fit to advise him to desist from
further prosecuting his designs, and to return
to his native country, where he shall enjoy

1 Col. Papers : Vol. V., No. 27.

2 Dated at Whitehall, Nov. 22, 1629. Col. Papers : Vol. V., No. 39.

such respects as his former services and late endeavours justly deserve.

But Lord Baltimore refused to accept King Charles's advice, and persisted in his request for a grant on the Continent of America. At length the King acceded to his request, and made him a grant of the province of Maryland; but before the patent could be drawn up, poor Lord Baltimore died. The patent, however, was made out and signed in favour of his son, Cecil, 2nd Lord Baltimore, on the 20th June, 1632.[1]

About the same time, the King issued his orders to the Canada Commissioners, to take possession of the forts then under the command of Lewis Kirke, and deliver them up to the French, according to his Royal word and pleasure. Having seen their authority, Lewis Kirke delivered up the forts to the Commissioners, and then returned to England to his brother's house, there to consider their mutual losses.

1 Colonial Entry Book : No. 52, p. 1—19.

In the year 1635, Lewis Kirke was appointed to the command of the " Leopard," and his brother Thomas to the command of the " Sampson," two men-of-war attached to the Channel Squadron. In the following year, he was removed to the " Repulse," and Thomas Kirke to the " Swallow," both ships in the same squadron. On the 20th August, 1636, the Repulse was invaded by a dreadful plague. Thirty sick men were landed at Margate, and eight more were left on board too ill to move. The surgeon lay dead " of spotted fever full of spots ;" so the Repulse was put out of commission and discharged.

Sir David Kirke, having tried every means to obtain redress for the injuries he had received, and convinced that nothing could be got from the French, not even the money which they had agreed to pay him, began to entertain the idea of taking up the colony at Newfoundland, which Lord Baltimore had deserted. He applied to the King for this purpose, and obtained from him on the 13th of November, 1637, a grant of the whole island of Newfoundland, with all the powers of a Count Palatine over the island.[1]

Sir David Kirke was not a man to waste his time,. so having collected 100 men to accompany him to Newfoundland, he fitted out one of his own ships, the "Abigail," with everything necessary for a colony, and sailed from England in the spring of 1638. He established himself at Ferryland in the

---

1 There is considerable difficulty with regard to this Grant to Sir David Kirke. On the 13th of November, 1637, two patents were drawn up and signed ; the first was a Grant to "Air right trustie and righte well-beloved cosens and counsellors, James, Marquess of Hamilton, Master of our Horse; Philip, Earle of Pembroke and Montgomerie, Lord Chamberlayne of our Household ; and Henrie, Earl of Holland, Chiefe Justice, Justice in Eyre of all our forests, chaces, and parkes in the southern side of our river of Trente; and to our well-beloved Sir David Kirke, Knight, one of the Gentlemen of our Privie Chamber," of "all that whole continent island or region, commonly called or knowne by the name of Newfoundlande, bordering upon the continente of America, &c., &c." The whole Grant is most absolute of every thing and right in that country. The second Grant is similar to the first, but is to Sir David Kirke only. It is impossible to account for these apparently contradictory Grants except upon the supposition that Sir David, being the only one of the grantees who intended to reside at Newfoundland, it was thought desirable to give him plenary powers in case any dispute should arise upon the island. He was also appointed by the other grantees Sole-Governor and Captain of the vast territory which they jointly possessed; and as his three co-grantees died in a few years, Sir David was left in sole possession.

M

house built by Lord Baltimore, and made every arrangement for a prolonged stay in the island. Before he left England, Sir David had formed a company to carry on the New-foundland trade. The Marquis of Hamilton, the Earl of Pembroke and Montgomery, and the Earl of Holland, had joined with him to form a company, and had assisted him with money to carry it out. Ships were sent out to the island, which were put under the management of Sir David, and the fish and oil which they collected, were forwarded to London, and sold by the company's manager in London.

Lord Baltimore's complaints and the dismal accounts which he had forwarded to England, had somewhat prejudiced men's minds against settling in the island: so one of the first acts of Sir David Kirke was to try and remove the injurious impressions which were afloat. For this purpose he wrote a long and highly interesting account of the country, with the prospects of trade in the different

industries then practised, which he divides
into eight heads—fishing, buying and making
of salt, making potashes, brewing and baking,
ironworks, impositions (taxes) upon strangers,
and trade. By the last head is meant barter
and traffic with the natives; and *apropos* to
this Sir David gives an interesting account of
former dealings with the natives, from which
I have quoted largely in my account of
Alderman Guy's expedition. In the conclusion of his narrative he ridicules the idea put
forward that noblemen and gentlemen should
not engage in trade, and that if they did
would be sure to lose their money. He says,
" Mala mens, malus animus. He that hath
a habit of playing false himself thinks every
man els a cheater. But wee knowe not the
condition and quality of the Answeares and
therefore wee will not be definitive in our cen-
sure as they are in their conclusion. It was
never heard, say they, that any lord or gentleman gott anything by tradinge. Never heard?
Hath noe man ever heard of the noblemen

and gentlemen of Italy? Have they noe
hand in merchandize? Nay, are not the
greatest of their princes some way or other
ingaged in a constant cause of traffique? But,
not to send you soe farr for examples, it is
very well knowne that divers gentlemen of
the west of England have for many yeares
past, and doe yet, to their great profit, continue even this trade of fishinge, the subject
of our discourse, which, if you had studyed
with a little more care and inquiry, you might
yet further have heard or read the opinions
and instructions upon such a theme, of a man
as great as any of his age brought forth, and
a great and eminent peere of England, who
adviseth in business of this nature to admitt
of none but noblemen and gentlemen, exclud-
ing utterly the merchant from having any
hand in the designe. Our hopes, therefore,
are that their Lordships will take the strange
encouragement to proceed in the course be-
gane, from the weakness of the reasons objected against it. And wee assure ourselves

wee shall render to the adventurers such accounts as shall give them high satisfaction, if in the manage of the business they be pleased to take the advice of such as have the best opportunityes to understand it. And are here for this purpose to doe all right to them, honour to His Majesty, and good to the natives of the land and all His Highnesses subjects that shall engage themselves in the action."

After a year's experience of Newfoundland, Sir David wrote home a most promising account of the country. He pronounces the climate to be healthy, though rather severe, the air agreeing with everyone, except Jesuits and schismatics—a sly rap at Lord Baltimore. Sir David had an equal dislike to both Catholics and Puritans: he was a good Churchman, and an admirer of Archbishop Laud, with whom he kept up a regular correspondence. One of his letters is extant, and as it gives a good account of his position, I shall insert it in full:—

" Most Reverend Father,

" I doe with joye and a gratefull hart, acknowledge the favour I received from your
Grace, in your good wishes for our prosperity
in this country, after it had pleased His
Majesty to grant to us by his Patent. My
Lord, I doubt not but God hath blessed us
the more for your Grace's blessing upon us,
for wee have found the country so good and
healthfull, that since our arrival heer, of
about 100 persons which wee brought over to
this daye, wee have lost but one of sickness,
and hee a diseased man, before we departed
out of England. Concerning the temperature
of the clyme, and the general estate of y°
country, your Grace may be at large informed
by these relations which are sent over to the
Company, and shall bee presented to your
Grace, if your more serious and greate imployments maye allowe any time of leysure
for their perusal. I shall only add this one
particular observation, out of what had happened in the country heretofore, and what I

hope shall followe hereafter. That the ayre
of Newfoundland agrees perfectly well with
all God's creatures, except Jesuits and schismatics. A great mortality amongst the former tribe so affrighted my Lord Baltimore,
that hee utterly deserted the country. And
of the other sort we have heard so many
frensies from our next neighbouring plantation, the greatest His Majesty hath in America,
that wee hope our strict observance and use
of the rites and service of the Church of
England, as it is our chiefest safety, by the
blessing of God, whose ordinance wee are
constantly persuaded it is. So may it dis-
courage for ever all seditious spirits to mingle
with us, to the disturbance of that happy
conformity which wee desire may be established in this land. To this good end, if it
shall please your Grace to give us directions
for the time to come (for we doubt not that
the country may be peopled in a short time
with a numerous plantation of His Majesty's
subjects), wee shall with all respect and

faythfulness receive and practise your Grace's injunctions: and I in my particular, shall rest ever,

"Your Grace's most obedient,

"DAVID KIRKE.[1]

"Ferryland, Octobris 2°, 1639.

"To the Most Reverend Father in God, William, by the Divine Providence, Lord Archbishop of Canterburie, his Grace present these."

Undismayed by the difficulties which had driven away Lord Baltimore, and determined to establish the Colony of Newfoundland upon a sure and lasting footing, Sir David Kirke laboured with all his might to develop the fisheries under his control; feeling, and that truly, that the mainland was too cold and barren ever to succeed as an agricultural colony, and that its whole wealth and importance depended upon the valuable fisheries which its seas afforded on every side. With

1 Col. Papers : Vol. X., No. 40. Endorsed by Laud, "Recd., Jan. 1640."

this idea, he used every effort to increase the
fishing trade, now grown to great importance,
by offering every facility to both British and
foreign fishermen to prosecute their trade—
both by means of his protection as Governor,
and also by erecting sheds on the land where
they could dry and salt their fish, and lodging
homes, where they could be housed and fed
during their sojourn in Newfoundland.   But
it could not be supposed that the British
fishermen would view with favour Kirke's
impartiality to all the fishermen who resorted
to the banks.   Murmurs were heard from them
on all sides, which at last formed coherent
expression in a petition to the Privy Council,
signed by the Bishop of Exeter, William
Peterson, and fourteen others, saying that
numerous complaints had been received from
merchants, fishermen, and others, of injuries
which they had received at the hands of Sir
David Kirke and his company.   " Cook rooms
and stages have been destroyed, and the
principal places for fishermen disposed of to

aliens. Taverns, which had been expressly forbidden by the Privy Council, have been set up by Kirke, whereby the fishermen waste their estates, and grow disorderly. It is requested that some timely course may be taken for the prevention of such houses."[1]

This petition was presented in January, 1640. In the following March, letters were sent by the Lords of the Privy Council to Sir David Kirke, informing him of the charges made against him. In September, Sir David writes[2] to the Privy Council. He protests that all the allegations are false. That the stages and cook-rooms have been pulled down by the fishermen themselves, inasmuch that the masters complained to him of these outrages. Has sent warrants to all planters and fishermen, to see the clauses of the 9th of His Majesty's reign duly kept. Hopes by good proofs to clear himself from causeless clamours against him. "Whoever

---

1 Col. Papers : Vol. X., No. 46.

2 Dated, "Ferryland, September 12, 1640." See Appendix F. and Col. Papers : Vol. X., No. 77.

would interrupt the fishing of Newfoundland,
is worthy the name of a traitor."

After this letter, we hear no more complaints against Sir David Kirke; either the
proofs which he offered of his innocence were
considered satisfactory, or else the civil war
which began in the following year, drove all
such trifling matters from the heads of both
King and Council.

During the next ten years—1640-50—there
is a great blank in the State Papers relating
to Newfoundland. The King and the Parliament were too much occupied with home
affairs to pay any attention to the state of
the Colonies, so that these last were left to
their own devices, some having espoused the
King's cause, and others that of the Parliament. Sir David Kirke, during this period,
remained in undisturbed possession of Newfoundland, and kept the Royal standard con-
tinually hoisted in front of his house and fort
of Ferryland. At the outbreak of the war,
his brothers, Lewis and Thomas, joined the

King when he hoisted his standard at Nottingham, on the 22nd of August, 1642, and Lewis Kirke was invested with the command of a troop of horse. Both the brothers fought in the bloody and undecisive battle of Edgehill; and not long afterwards, Thomas Kirke was killed in one of the numerous skirmishes which took place between the Cavaliers and Roundheads. Lewis Kirke accompanied the King into the West of England, took part in the siege of Gloucester, which was raised by the Earl of Essex, and in the battle of Newbury. Here he so distinguished himself, that a few days after the battle, he was knighted[1] by the King at Oxford, whither the Royal army had retired, on the 23rd of April, 1643. He was afterwards made Governor of Bridgnorth Castle, in the county of Shropshire, a place of considerable strength and importance, which fact we learn from two letters, one written by the King to Sir Lewis Kirke, from Evesham, ordering him to send

---

1 See Harleian MS., 6062; Landsdowne MS., 807, f. 62.

some victuals for the army, and the other
from Sir Lewis Kirke[1] to Sir Francis Ottley,
upon the same business. From this time we
lose sight of Sir Lewis Kirke, until the Restoration, when he was appointed Captain and
Paymaster of the Corps of Gentlemen-at-Arms.
That he continued to fight for the King until
his cause was hopeless there can be no doubt,
especially as we find his name down in the
list of delinquents, compelled to pay from his
slender purse £151 for his loyalty to his
King.[2]

1 Letter of Sir Lewis Kirke, Governor of Bridgnorth Castle, to Sir
Francis Ottley : "Sir,—His Majestie being advanced to Evesham, hath
by His letters from thence of the VIth instanty, required me speedilie
to provide and send ten tonne of cheese from these parts to be delivered
to the Mayor of Worcester, who shall give the owners satisfaction out
of the markett rates. I desire you, therefore, that you send in this
night, soe soon after as possible, yn care to Bayliffe Synge's house at
Bridgnorth, one tonne of a good sorte of cheese, whether ould or this
yeare's making, and thence that there be an officer appointed to receive
the same, and to attend itt to Worcester, and to demand to receive the
monies for itt there, which shall, upon his return, bee speedilie paid
everie person who shall soe send in. Letting you further know, that as
I have sent unto His Majestie an account how I have proceeded in his
commands, by sending him a catalogue of the names of the persons and
ₜhe portions from them required, see I must if there be a fail in any
one, and signifie the same to His Majestie, for my owne excuse. I rest
your loveing friend to serve you,   "LEWIS KIRKE."

2 If we are to believe a petition to King Charles II. by Colonel

In the meanwhile, Sir David Kirke held Newfoundland for the King, and offered His Majesty an asylum in that place, when England was no longer safe for him to stay in. With a view to maintaining his position, Sir David procured 400 seamen from England, by offering high pay, and other advantages, to man his ships, which he also armed with heavy guns. These men were brought from England under the pretence of filling vacancies in the fishing ships at Newfoundland; but the affair having got wind, the Council of State issued an ordinance on the 23rd of February, 1649, to the Comptrollers of Customs

Temple, in December, 1660, one of the Kirkes accompanied King Charles I. upon the scaffold. In this petition (to be found in the Col. Papers : Vol. XIV., No. 64) Colonel Temple says, "One of the last commands that he (the King) whispered to Kirke on the scaffold was to charge this King to have a care of honest Tom Temple." Though Col. Temple may have been mistaken about this last injunction of the unfortunate King, yet the very fact of his asserting that it was said to Kirke, proves that one of that name must have been present on the scaffold at the execution, as the event was quite recent enough, and being of such great importance to leave every fact imprinted on the minds of the spectators. Who this Kirke could be we have no means of knowing; it must, however, have been one of two persons, either Sir Lewis Kirke, the distinguished cavalier, or else George Kirke, groom of the bedchamber, most probably the latter.

at Plymouth, Dartmouth, and Barnstaple, re-
quiring them not to let any more sailors to
go to Newfoundland, as they are informed
that 400 seamen have been taken up under
pretence of being transported to Newfoundland, to fish for Sir David Kirke, and that
by reason of the great wages, and other advantages offered, the navy of the Commonwealth could not be furnished with men.

The death of the King frustrated Sir David's
intentions; but determined to hold out as
long as possible, he wrote to Prince Rupert,
who about this time was cruising in the
English Channel, with a fleet which had re-
volted from the Parliament, and begged him
to make sail for Newfoundland, where he
could recruit his fleet, and devise fresh schemes
for annoying the enemy.[1] Upon the receipt
of this message, Prince Rupert set sail for
America; but news of his intention had been
conveyed to London, and a fleet, under the

1 Interregnum Entry Book : Vol. XC., p. 263. Ibid : Vol. CXV.
p. 148.

command of Sir George Ayscue, was sent to prevent his joining Sir David Kirke at New-foundland; so diverting his course, he made all sail for Barbadoes, which enjoyed the reputation of being the most loyal of the Colonies.

The battle had been fought out, and now the victors were engaged in dividing the spoil. Sequestrators were sent into all the counties of England to take inventories of all the property of delinquents, and appropriate the same to the uses of the Commonwealth. Of the owners some had fallen in battle, the rest had fled to Holland, France, and the colonies, to escape death or imprisonment. In this universal spoliation it was not to be expected Sir David Kirke would escape: he was known to be a zealous royalist, his brothers had done good service in the King's armies, and he had recently been discovered in treaty with the enemy. But still his case was not an ordinary one; he owed no allegiance to the English Parliament; by his grant he ex-

ercised palatinate jurisdiction over Newfoundland and its dependencies (the other grantees
being by this time all dead), and he himself
had not taken up arms against the Parliament.
It was, therefore, thought advisable by the
Government to rake up the old grievances
which had been alleged against him by the
Western traders before the outbreak of the
war, and to cite him to answer these charges.
On the 8th of April, 1651, a warrant was
issued to Captain Thomas . Thoroughgood,
commander of the "Crescent," to sail to Newfoundland, and bring Sir David Kirke to
England, to answer the charges which have
been made against him.[1] But to show how
little justice Kirke could expect at the hands
of the Government, a warrant was issued on
the same day to John Treworgie and Walter
Sykes, ordering them to sail in the Crescent
to Newfoundland, and to sequestrate, for the
benefit of the Commonwealth, all ordnance,
ammunition, houses, boats, and other articles

1 Interregnum Entry Book : Vol. CXVII. p. 114.

N

belonging to Sir David Kirke, and to collect the
taxes paid by strangers for the right of fishing.

Sir David arrived in England in September,
and immediately presented himself before the
Council, anxious that a most thorough inves-
tigation of his conduct should be made.

But now began a series of most vexatious
delays. The 4th of November was appointed
by order of the Council to consider the business relating to Newfoundland, but though
Sir David attended with his papers, nothing
was done. On the 12th of January, 1652,
an order of the Council was issued appointing
Mr. Nevile, the Earl of Pembroke, Colonel
Morley, Mr. Love, Colonel Purefoy, Mr. Hay,
Mr. Holland, Mr. Scott, Mr. Bond, and Sir
Arthur Haselrig, or any three of them, a Committee to examine the business concerning Sir
David Kirke, to peruse papers relative to his
doings in Newfoundland, and to require an
account of what is due to the Commonwealth
on the profits of shares forfeited to the state,
and to report upon the whole matter.[1]

1 Interregnum Entry Book : Vol. XCIV., pp. 192, 272, 280.

On the 29th of the same month, Sir David
Kirke was summoned before the Council, and
ordered to enter into a bond not to depart out
of the Commonwealth, and to be in readiness
to attend the Committee when sent for. He
was always ready to meet the Committee, but
the Committee did not seem equally anxious
to meet him. As if the Committee was not
already large enough, Sir Henry Vane, Mr.
Masham, Mr. Challoner, Colonel Dixwell, Mr.
Corbett, Lord Bradshaw, and Mr. Morley
were added to it by order of Council, dated
April 2nd.[1] On the 12th of the same month,
Sir David presented a petition to the Council,
praying that his case might be entered into;
but it was not till the 11th of June that his
case was heard. The result of their delibera-
tions was to the effect that Sir David Kirke
had no authority in Newfoundland under the
grant of Charles Stuart; that all forts, houses,
stages, and other appurtenances relating to
the fishing trade, and established on the island

1 Interregnum Entry Book : Vol. XCIV., p. 533.

by Kirke and his fellow-adventurers, should be
forfeited to the Government as the property
of delinquents; that Kirke's own private effects
shall be secured to him, and he is to be at
liberty to send over his wife and servants to
take care of his estate.[1]   At the same time
instructions were sent to Walter Sykes, Robert
Street, Captain William Pyle, and Captain
Nicholas Redwood, commissioners for manag-
ing and ordering the affairs and interest of
the Commonwealth in Newfoundland in the
year ensuing, "to repair thither immediately,
and take possession of the ordnance, ammunition, houses, boats, stages, and other appurtenances belonging to the fishing trade; to collect
impositions until Parliament declare their
further pleasure. Take care for the government and well-ordering of the inhabitants;
secure the fishery against Rupert or any others;
discover what is due to the Commonwealth
upon the adventure of several delinquents, and

1 Interregnum Entry Book: Vol. CLIX., p. 7. Ibid: Vol. LVII.,
pp. 11, 14, 22, 24.

alleged to be in the hands of Sir David Kirke, who is to be permitted by himself or deputies to manage his estate there, subject to rules and directions from themselves; to administer the engagement to all the inhabitants; give a full account of their proceedings from time to time; admit Sir David Kirke to cross-examine witnesses; and enquire into complaints."

At the same time, permission was granted to Sir David to return to Newfoundland, on condition that he returned to England with the Commissioners, and in the meanwhile gave security that he would answer whatever was objected against him, and to pay such sums as shall appear to be due from him to the Commonwealth. Upon such hard terms as these, Sir David Kirke returned to his estates at Ferryland, in the summer of 1652. He could not have remained long there, for in the spring of 1653, we find him again in England, for a petition of his to the Council of State, was filed on the 4th of March,

1653,[1] and on the 30th of the same month, Sir David and Mr. Sykes, the Commissioner, were ordered to appear before the Council, on the 1st of April; upon which day Sir David appeared, but Mr. Sykes, making default, the latter was peremptorily ordered to attend on the 15th instant, on which day the petitions on both sides were considered, and the business referred to the Committee for Foreign Affairs.

Sir David, in the meanwhile, had not been idle. He had gained the assistance of Colonel Claypole, Cromwell's son-in-law, by making him a present of a large estate in Newfoundland, and promising him a share of the fishery duties. With Claypole's assistance, he obtained the removal of the sequestration upon his property, and with the exception of the ordnance and forts, the whole was restored to him; and he was allowed to return to Newfoundland, upon en-

1 Interregnum Entry Book: Vol. CLXI., pp. 15, 16, 20, 23, 26, 29, 32, 33.

tering into a bond of double the value of his
estate, to answer any charges that might be
brought against him.[1]

With such terms, which were the best he
could procure, Kirke was bound to be satisfied;
so he set sail for Newfoundland, and arrived
there in the autumn of 1653.   At this time
his troubles seemed to be over, and he might
with reason look forward to a life of happiness and usefulness, in the wild, but interesting country, in which he had established
himself.   Through all the latter period of his
life, through cloud and sunshine, he had been
sustained by the assistance of a devoted and
loving wife.   Children had been born to him,
and his house at Ferryland was filled with
stalwart sons and fair daughters, who would,
as he hoped, in after years uphold the honour
of his house, and extend its influence in the
land where he had been for so many years
little short of an independent sovereign.

But all these hopes and expectations were

1 Interregnum Entry Book: Vol. XCVII., pp. 197, 204—7.

blighted by his death, which took place in
the winter of 1655-6, but the exact date is
not known. His end was sudden and un-
expected, as he was only in his 56th year.
Naturally he was of a robust constitution; but
trouble and anxiety, and the exposure for many
years to the rigour of an extremely cold climate,
must have made him prematurely old, and
laid the seeds of the disease which eventually
carried him off, at a comparatively early age.[1]

No account of Sir David Kirke, by the hand
of a contemporary, has come down to us, but
if we may judge him by his actions, he was
certainly an extraordinary person. He was
essentially a practical man; his theories were
never stultified by his actions, and his success
in most cases, certainly in those which depended upon his own exertions, far exceeded
his expectations. But throughout his life he
was most unfortunate in all his undertakings.
Never were the achievements of an English

1 The exact date of his death is uncertain; but in a petition of
Walter Sykes to the Privy Council, on the 29th April, 1656, Sir David
is spoken of as deceased, so he must have died in the winter of 1655-6.

officer more unrequited. The capture of
Canada and Nova Scotia, the destruction of
a French fleet of eighteen sail, and the expenditure of £40,000, was ill rewarded by
an empty title, and an honorary addition to
his arms. But instead of being discouraged
and disgusted, his ill success in the Canadas
only spurred on Sir David to fresh exertions;
he was the only man of his time who fully
appreciated the value of the Newfoundland
fisheries; and, undeterred by the ill success
which attended Lord Baltimore, Dr. Vaughan,
and others, who had attempted to colonize
Newfoundland, he determined to risk his life
and estate in a similar attempt.

We have seen how he succeeded. For
nearly twenty years he resided at Ferryland
as Governor, and during the latter period, as
sole owner of the whole island. He pro-
tected the fisheries from pirates, and in return
gained a considerable revenue, in the shape
of a tax paid for the use of stages on the
sea shore, erected for the purpose of drying

the fish caught. During the civil war in England, both the King and the Parliament were too much occupied with home affairs, to give any thought to those of Newfoundland; so Sir David was left in sole possession of the island, responsible to none, though he himself, as a staunch supporter of the King, considered himself under His Majesty's commands, until the unfortunate monarch had ceased to live.

The death of the King was the signal for his own ruin. As a malignant, his estates were confiscated, he himself summoned to England, and put under arrest, though afterwards liberated upon giving enormous bail, and although at last permitted to return to Newfoundland, it was as a ruined man.

But though he was prevented carrying out his plans to their fullest extent, the sojourn of Sir David Kirke in Newfoundland was productive of the greatest benefit to the island, and laid the foundation of its subsequent prosperity.

He left three sons, who were all with him in Newfoundland at the time of his death: George, David, and Philip. Upon the Restoration, Sir Lewis Kirke, their uncle, presented a petition to the King on their behalf, reciting his own services in the Civil War, the services of his brother, and the grant to Sir David Kirke, by King Charles I., of the island of Newfoundland, and praying that the ships about to be sent thither, may assist his nephews to recover their inheritance, of which they had been dispossessed.[1] But, as is well known, Charles II. found himself much embarrassed at his Restoration' between two conflicting parties. There were the old Cavaliers, who had fought and bled for his father on many a field of battle, and there were his new friends, the Presbyterians, and moderate party, who, disgusted with the tyranny of the party under Cromwell, and the extravagancies of religious madmen, had restored him to the throne of his ancestors. It

1 Col. Papers : Vol. XIV., No. 8.

was a hard position to be placed in, and no wonder many old and tried friends of monarchy had to suffer under the plea of expediency.

Cecil, Lord Baltimore, put in a claim to Newfoundland, under the grant to his father, by James I. As we have seen, there can be no doubt the first Lord Baltimore abandoned Newfoundland; in his letter to King Charles, he prays to be removed from the island, and to have a grant of land where the climate was less rigorous. This request was granted by Charles, and he made over to Lord Baltimore the territory of Maryland.

In the full conviction that the Baltimores had abandoned Newfoundland, Sir David Kirke obtained a grant of that place from the King, and in this grant it is recited that, " George, Lord Baltimore, having left the plantation in no sort provided for, Cecil, his heir, having also deserted it, as have several others who have grants of parcels of land, leaving divers of our poor subjects in the said province, living without government, this grant was made at the humble petition[1] of the above."

This was in 1637, and no complaint was made by Lord Baltimore till 1660. It is difficult to see, then, what claims he could substantiate. However, he prevailed with the Council, and the King issued a warrant to Sir Lewis Kirke,[1] Elizabeth, widow of Sir David Kirke, and his sons, Philip, George, and David, to deliver up possession of all their property in Newfoundland, as it belonged to Lord Baltimore, by the grant of James I. to his father.

1 In the grant to Sir David Kirke it is specially recited, "But the said Lord Baltimore deserting the sayd plantation in his life tyme, and leavinge the same in noe sorte provided for, accordinge to the sayd undertakinge, and yet leavinge divers of our poore subjects in the sayd province livinge without government, the sayd Lord Baltimore shortlie afterwards died; and Cecile, his sonne and heire apparent, hath alsoe deserted the sayd province and plantation, and alsoe Sir Frauncis Bacon, Knighte, deceased, afterwards Lord Albons, and late Lord Chauncellor of England, our citie of London, and divers others to whom severall graunts of divers parcells of Newfoundland aforesayd were alsoe, by severall letters patent, formerly graunted, have alsoe deserted the province and plantation."

2 Col. Papers : Vol. XIV., No. 9 (2).

Deprived of their rights in Newfoundland,
Sir Lewis and his brother John attempted to
recover the money which the French had
agreed to pay to them and their brother David
for the forts in Canada and Nova Scotia. On
the 19th of July, 1660, a petition was presented by them to the Committee for Foreign
Plantations, in which they state that "they were
with others settled in Nova Francia, Acadia,
and Canada, from 1628 to 1632, and expended
almost £60,000 in improving the plantations
and trade in those parts; but were obliged by
the treaty of 1632 to withdraw themselves,
their servants, ships, and goods, and pay the
French £9000. Notwithstanding, none of the
agreements have been performed by the
French, although the petitioners have presented their demands for redress, as also for
a ship taken in 1633. In 1655, the late pre-
tended Protector regained these forts and
places, and retained them upon the petitioners'
title, but refused their right because they were
malignants; and committed the benefit and

trade to Thomas Temple, in whose custody they now are. Pray that the several forts and places now in the hands of Temple may be given up to them, or detained till the French satisfy the petitioners, who can make it appear they are damnified above £53,000 sterling."[1]

But though several petitions were presented, and everything possible done, no money could be procured. The King was on too good terms with France to demand the payment of the £60,000; so the widow and children of Sir David Kirke were left poor and unprovided for, whilst Charles and his ministers reaped a rich harvest, the result of his exertions.

During Sir David Kirke's government of Newfoundland, he offered every inducement to colonists to settle in the island, so that before the year 1650 more than three hundred and fifty families were located in different parts of the island. After his death a petition was addressed by the inhabitants to the Lords

1 Col. Papers : Vol. XIV., No. 22, 23, 24, 28.

of Trade and Plantations,[1] applying for some
local governor and magistrates who should
decide disputes and prevent disorders amongst
them; but their sensible request was opposed
by the merchants and shipowners in London
and Bristol who were interested in the Newfoundland trade; and, strange to say, their
opposition was successful. The colonists again
renewed their petition to the King for a
governor in 1674; but instead of granting
their request, the Lords of Trade and Plantations advised His Majesty that all emigration
to Newfoundland should be discouraged, and
all existing plantations destroyed. His Majesty
was induced to approve of this extraordinary

---

1 Commission to Edward Hyde, Lord Chancellor; Thomas, Earl of
Southampton; Edward, Earl of Manchester; Theophilus, Earl of Lin-
coln; John, Earl of Clare; James, Earl of Marlborough; Jerome, Earl
of Portland; with Viscount Saye and Sele, and others. The King
judging it necessary that so many remote colonies and governments so
many ways considerable to our crown, should be brought under an uni-
form inspection and conduct for their future regulation, security, and
improvement, they are appointed a standing Council, with authority to
any five to take into their consideration the condition of the foreign
plantations according to instructions annexed. Power to appoint clerks,
messengers, &c., whose salaries are not to exceed £300 per annum.
Col. Papers : Vol. XIV., No. 59.

scheme, and under his authority the most wanton cruelties were practised upon the unfortunate settlers, to compel them to abandon their adopted country. In 1676, this cruel system was abolished, and His Majesty ordered that the settlers should be undisturbed. For some reason or another the colonization of Newfoundland was considered by the Government as detrimental to the fisheries, and everything was done to prevent emigration to the island. In 1697, the Board of Trade, after hearing both sides of the question, decided that not more than one thousand planters should be allowed to reside upon the island. During the war with Louis XIV. all our colonies in Newfoundland were captured by the enemy, except Bonavista and Carbonier, but they were all recovered by an English squadron.

I have now traced the history of Newfoundland from its earliest known period to the close of the 17th century; about which time it became a settled colony of the British em-

o

pire. A governor was granted at last to the
prayers of the inhabitants, and all the settlements on the island were joined together
under a wise and salutary organization.

CHAPTER V.

Nova Scotia after the Treaty of St. Germains—Expedition of Razillai—His death—Succeeded by M. Charnisé—Quarrels between Charnisé and De La Tour—The latter seeks aid from Boston—And from Sir David Kirke—Charnisé attacks Fort St. John—Its defence by Madame La Tour—Death of Charnisé—La Tour's success—Capture of Nova Scotia by Major Sedgwick—Granted to Thos. Temple, and others—Ceded to France in 1667.

As we saw in a former chapter, Acadia, or as it was called by the English, Nova Scotia, was ceded, together with Canada, to France by the treaty of St. Germains, from which treaty may be dated the commencement of a long train of calamities to the colonies and to England; the subsequent provincial disputes; and in some measure the success of the American Revolution. Razillai, with a large force, was sent by the King of France to take

possession of the country, carrying with him
a commission as commander-in-chief of the
colony, and a grant of the river and bay of
St. Croix. The remainder of the province was
divided between Claude de la Tour, who had
obtained a grant from Sir William Alexander,
and Mons. Denys. La Tour applied to the
French King for a confirmation of his grant,
which was allowed with the addition of the
islands of Sable and La Have. Razillai died
soon after his arrival at Nova Scotia, and M.
Charnisè was appointed as his successor. This
officer quarrelled with La Tour about the
division of their land, and so violent did their
animosity rage, that Louis the XIIIth wrote
to them with his own hand in the hope of
settling their differences. But his letter had
not the desired effect; both parties renewed
their complaints to the King; and Charnisè,
in consequence of the unfavourable account
which he was able to give of his adversary,
obtained an order to arrest him and send him
prisoner to France. Both parties being about

equal in strength, La Tour defied his adversary; and sailing to Boston, begged for aid
from the colony of Massachusetts. The
Puritans living there, according to their custom consulted their Bibles on the subject;
and though some contended that it was lawful
for them to succour him as Joshua helped the
Gibeonites against the other Canaanites, and
Jehosaphat aided Jehoram against Moab, the
majority were of opinion that the speech of
the prophet to Jehosaphat, in the 2nd Chron.,
19th chap., and 2nd verse, actually forbade
them to help him.

During La Tour's absence at Boston, his
fort of St. John was attacked by Charnisè
with a considerable force. He expected to make
it an easy conquest, but it was defended by
Madame la Tour with a heroism equal to
that displayed a few years later by Charlotte
de la Tremouille at Lathom House; so that
Charnisè was glad to offer terms of honourable
capitulation, which were accepted by the lady.
No sooner, however, had he become master

of the fort, than, with excessive barbarity, he hung all the prisoners, and compelled Madame la Tour to witness the butchery with a halter round her neck.

She soon afterwards died, and La Tour, in desperation, fled to Newfoundland, to implore aid from Sir David Kirke; but failing to get any help from him, he seemed for a time to have abandoned any attempt to recover his possessions. During his wanderings, he was suddenly recalled by news of the death of Charnisè, which took place in 1651. Hastening back to St. John, this extraordinary man seized upon Madame Charnisè, married her off hand, and obtained at the same time from Charnisè's sister, a renunciation of her claim to her brother's lands, and settled himself at last as sole owner of Nova Scotia. But he was not now left in peace; M. le Borgne, a creditor of Charnisè, accused La Tour to King Lewis as a heretic, and obtained a decree in France, authorizing him to enter upon the lands of the deceased debtor.

Armed with this power, he sailed to Nova
Scotia, attacked and burnt La Have, and
was making preparations for the seizure of
Port Royal, when his career was stopped
by the English. Cromwell, who with all his
faults, upheld the honour of England abroad,
had determined to recover Nova Scotia. So
he despatched in 1654, an armed force under
the command of Major Sedgwick. Having
attacked and defeated La Tour, the English
attacked Le Borgne at Port Royal, and
though he had a strong garrison, a numerous
artillery, and plenty of provisions, quickly
compelled him to surrender.

La Tour, nothing daunted by the change
of events, immediately availed himself of the
English protection, quietly laid claim to his
estates, and petitioned the Protector, in con-
junction with Thomas Temple and William
Crome, for a grant of Nova Scotia. He
drew up a statement of his claim under the
grant of Sir William Alexander to his father,
and was so far successful, that on the 9th

August, 1656, he obtained a grant by letters patent, under the great seal, granting to himself, under the title of Sir Charles La Tour, Thomas Temple, and William Crome, the whole country of Nova Scotia.[1]

Mr. Temple, afterwards Sir Thomas Temple, purchased La Tour's share, and immediately established the several colonies which had been begun by the French. He also ex-

---

1 Warrant for articles of agreement between Oliver, Lord Protector, and Sir Charles St. Stephen, Lord de la Tour, Baronet of Scotland; Thomas Temple, and William Crome, to pass the great seal. Letters patent to be granted on or before the 10th of August next for all those lands in America called Acadia, and that part of the country called Nova Scotia, the boundaries of which are particularly described, with reservation of lands already granted to any colony in New England. Prohibition of trade with the savages to all others without license, and power to seize vessels so employed. Twenty moose skins and twenty beaver skins to be rendered yearly to the Lord Protector or his successors; also the sum of £1812 due to officers and soldiers since 15th of August, 1655, according to the establishment made by Robert Sedgwick, Major-General of the forces there. Governors to be approved by commission under the Privy or Great Seal of England; ordnance, ammunition, and martial stores to be preserved for the service of the state and security of the forts; commodities arising by trade with the natives to be sent to the United Kingdom to be free from custom or import; Margaret, the relict of Major Edward Gibbons, to be paid £379 11s., owing heretofore, upon the mortgage of Fort St. John, by De la Tour, who, with Temple and Crome, agreed to give security for the performance of all the agreements in this covenant. Endorsed, J. Lisle. Recorded, 16th July, 1656. Col. Papers: Vol. XIII, No. 4.

pended £16,000 in repairing the forts, and soon received a large income from the fur and fishery trades. But Temple was not left undisturbed in his money making. He finds the country not quite to his taste. In a pathetic letter to a friend, he thanks him "for the great love and care that could find him out even in the deserts of America, whither his unhappy lot had led him;" and in May, 1658, he was attacked by a Monsieur Laborne, who invaded the country, seized the fort of La Have, and all the goods therein belonging to Temple. Upon a summons to surrender the fort, Laborne killed Captain Story and two others, and wounded many more. He was captured and brought prisoner to Boston, and being interrogated about his conduct, confessed that his only reason for such extraordinary behaviour, was that his father had gone to England to obtain a grant of Nova Scotia from the Protector, and he thought he might be improving the time by occupying a few places for his father until his triumphant return.

A company had been formed in England to carry on the trade in Nova Scotia, of which Lord Fienes was chairman.[1] This company materially assisted Temple in developing the resources of the country. But all their efforts were thrown away, as the English Government, in the same year in which they endeavoured to drive away the inhabitants of Newfoundland, again surren-

[1] Agreement of the Company of Nova Scotia for carrying on a trade there. Captain Middleton to be sent over as agent for the Company, to treat with Colonel Thomas Temple, Lieutenant-Governor, for settling a trade there. To be furnished with merchandise to the value of £800, which is to be raised by the subscriptions of Lords Fienes and Wolseley, Martin Noell, Thomas Povey, and others. Each subscriber of £100 to have equal management and interest. Captains Watts and Collier to be desired to be husbands to the Company. Col. Papers : Vol. XIII., No. 43.

Minute of articles deposed by Captain Breedon, on the part of Colonel Thomas Temple, Lieutenant-Governor of Nova Scotia, to Lord Fienes, and others, the Company of Adventurers, for settling a trade in those parts ; the course first designed by the Adventurers not being thought convenient. The Company to advance a stock of £10,000. Colonel Temple to be allowed £500 per annum, with other privileges, which, with those to be enjoyed by the Company, are detailed. It is desired by the Company that a treaty may be forthwith concluded with the French Ambassador, for settlement of all pretences to Nova Scotia, or if that be refused, that the English may have power to invade the French in their possessions in that country. The French remaining at Port Royal by treaty, to submit to the Government of his Highness, or quit their farms, and be transported elsewhere. Col. Papers : Vol. XIII., No. 64.

dered Nova Scotia to the French, by the
Treaty of Breda in 1667.[1] It is beyond the

1 The Treaty of Breda was signed by Charles in great haste, to close
a war which had proved singularly disastrous to England. De Ruyter
had destroyed an English fleet, sailed up the Thames, and threatened
London with a bombardment. England would have fared ill but for
the energetic assistance of Lewis, who marched a large army into
Flanders, and frightened the Dutch Government into accepting fair
terms of peace. As the price of his interference, Lewis received Nova
Scotia. In this transaction, as well as in the Treaty of St. Germains,
the English Government showed an utter disregard of the interests of
the Nova Scotian Settlers. By the first treaty, the French agreed to
pay Sir David Kirke £60,000 for the forts and ammunition in Nova
Scotia. This money had never been paid, though acknowledged as due
by the French Ambassador. The following papers will show the treatment which the unfortunate settlers received from both French and
English authorities :—

"Minutes concerning the title of Lord Stirling and of Thomas Temple
to Nova Scotia. Articles made between Sir Lewis Kirke and the
French King, in 1632, but not being performed, the Kirkes became
damnified £60,000. Lord Stirling (Sir William Alexander) parted with
his interest, and was to have received from King Charles £10,000 for it.
It is desired that it may be taken into consideration who has the best
title to the country."

"Petition of Colonel John Blount and Ladies Mary and Jane Alexander, daughters of the late Earl of Stirling, to the King. William, late
Earl of Stirling, having at vast expense planted a colony in Nova Scotia,
lost his whole fortune, when at the conclusion of peace it was restored
to the French. For his relief, the late King granted him £10,000 out
of the exchequer and profits of Scotland. The Earl died before payment was made, and the petitioner Blount, who married Dame Mary,
Countess of Stirling, has disbursed for her and her children, £2,500.
Pray for letters patent for satisfaction of the £10,000."

"Petition of Charles St. Stephen, Lord de la Tour, Baronet of Nova
Scotia, Thomas Temple, and William Cronne, to the Privy Council.
Set forth King James grant of 1621, to Lord Stirling, of all Nova

scope of this short work to pursue the history of Nova Scotia any further. We have traced the earliest settlements which were made upon the country, through their youthful history, and the only thoughts which we can derive from the contemplation of this, and the sister colonies of Canada and Newfoundland, are full of admiration for the energy and perseverance displayed by English merchants and adventurers, and of wonder at the culpable negligence of the home Government, that was ready at any time to surrender to the ambition of France, territories which had been won by the blood and money of Englishmen.

Scotia, with power to create Baronets there, confirmed by King Charles in 1625. Lord Stirling's grant of part of the country to De la Tour, who, with his father, first settled in the wilderness with the savages, 15 years before any grant was passed. Their quiet possession of those lands, until Major Sedgwick, in 1654, violently forced them out, and plundered them of their goods to the amount of £10,000. Right of Temple and Cronne, by purchase from De la Tour. Are informed that some one, knowing the true state of their right, have endeavoured to obtain a grant of Nova Scotia. Pray for permission to prove their title." Col. Papers: Vol. XIV., Nos. 57, 60, 64.

APPENDIX A.

So MUCH ignorance has been displayed by the various writers who have treated of North America as to the birth and parentage of Sir David Kirke, that I think it better in this place to prove their want of information, and also the truth of my own statements.

Haliburton, in his "History of Nova Scotia," vol. I., p. 45, speaks of him as "One, David Kirtch, who assisted Sir William Alexander in the recovery of Nova Scotia. This extraordinary person was a native of Dieppe, a French Calvinist, who sought refuge in England from religious persecution in France, and was commonly called Sir David Kirke." Macgregor, in his "History of British America," says (vol. II., p. 21), "In 1632, Sir William Alexander, assisted by a French

Calvinist of the name of Kirckt, who fled to
England from Dieppe, in France, on the score
of religious persecution, fitted out a few vessels,
well armed, for Nova Scotia. This squadron,
commanded by Kirckt, who was also made a
baronet, under the title of Sir David Kirk."

It will be seen at once that these are utter
mistakes. Sir David Kirke was a knight and
not a baronet, and that he was of English
birth the following documents from the College
of Arms and elsewhere, will abundantly testify.

Funeral certificate of Mr. Gervase Kirke:—

" Mr. Jervays Kyrke, gentleman and mar-
chant of London, the sonne of Thurstan
Kyrke, of Greenhill, in the County of Derby,
departed this mortall life at his house in
Basing Lane, London, the xviith daye of
December, 1629, and was interred in the
parish church of Alhallows, in Bread Street,
the 22nd daye of the moneth following. He
married Elizabeth, daughter of John Gowding,
of Deepe, in France, where he had lyved the
most part of forty years, by whom he had

yssue five sonnes and two daughters. David
Kirke, eldest sonne, of the age of about thirty-
two years, captayne and chiefe commander
in a late fleete of nine sayle for the taking
of Canada, in the mayne lande of America;
in which expedition he soe worthely demeaned
himselfe, that he tooke the country, surprised
the French that had there planted and fortified
themselves, wone their forte, and tooke their
cheife commander prisoner, and brought him
captyve into England: Lewis Kirke, second
sonne, of the age of about thirty yeares, nowe
captayne and governor of the said fort for
His Majestie in Canada: Thomas Kirke, third
sonne, of the age of twenty-six years, captayne
and vice-admirall of the aforesaid fleet: John
Kirke, fourth sonne, of the age of twenty-three
years: and James, youngest sonne, of the age
of twenty-one years: Elizabeth, eldest
daughter, married to Jaques Greteuelo, a
Frenchman, in Deepe, by who she hath one
son, David Greteuilo, of the age of one year,
and one daughter, Elizabeth, of the age of

two yeares: Mary, youngest daughter of said defunct, of the age of ten yeares. He made Mrs. Elizabeth Kirke, his sayd wife, sole executrix of his last will and testament.

"This certificate was taken by Sampson Lennard, Blewmantle."

Extracted from the records of the

College of Arms, London,

ALBERT W. WOODS,

GARTER.

College of Arms,

    24th December, 1869.

PEDIGREE, EXTRACTED FROM BRITISH MUSEUM.—

Add. MS., 5533.

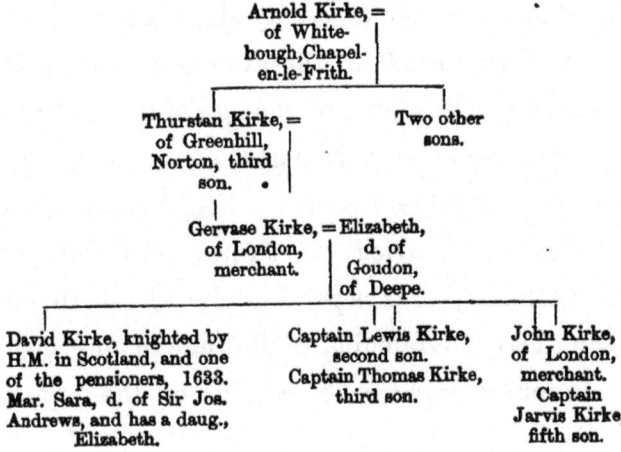

Arnold Kirke, = of White-hough, Chapel-en-le-Frith.

Thurstan Kirke, = of Greenhill, Norton, third son.

Two other sons.

Gervase Kirke, = Elizabeth, of London, merchant. d. of Goudon, of Deepe.

David Kirke, knighted by H.M. in Scotland, and one of the pensioners, 1633. Mar. Sara, d. of Sir Jos. Andrews, and has a daug., Elizabeth.

Captain Lewis Kirke, second son. Captain Thomas Kirke, third son.

John Kirke, of London, merchant. Captain Jarvis Kirke, fifth son.

APPENDIX B.

" To the Right Honourable the Lords of
H.M. most Honourable Privie Council.

" Whereas I received an order from your L͞pp
off the ninth of this instant, Aprill, concerning
the difference between .General de Caen and
the Merchant Adventurers of Canada, about
the beaver skinns in question between them.
I have sent for the said marchȧnts, the greatest
p͞te whereoft appeared before me at severall
times, and seemed to be willing that the said
General de Caen should have the said skinns
delivered unto him, according to your L͞pps'
said order, by the said Solomon Smith, Mar-
shall of the Admiralty; but amongst the rest
of the said marchants, Captaine Kirke, who,
as I am informed hath the custodie of one of
the keyes to each warehouse dore wherein

P

the skynnes are, although hee hath been dyvers tymes warned, never appeared before mee, who is either out of towne or else refuseth to be spoken withall, and as I p̄ceive the said skynnes will not be delivered unto the said Generall de Caen nor his assignees untill some further order be taken by your L̄pps, that the said Generall de Caen at his last being with mee informed mee that his occasions were such that he cold not staie in England untill such time as the difference, between him and the said marchants was ended, but wold appoynt one as his assignee to follow the said business in his behalf, in which place he hath appoynted one, Jaques Reynard, who appeared before mee and pretendeth his onlie staie in this kingdom is to see this business ended, which hee alledgeth is an extraordinary hindrance unto him in his affaires. All which I humbly . leave unto your L̄pps consideracon. This Twenty-eighth of Aprill, 1630.

JAMES CAMPBELL,

Mayor.

APPENDIX C.

ANSWEARES to five severall Memorialls, presented by the French Ambassador, to the Lords Committees for forrayne affaires, Feb. 1, 1629.

1. Concerning the restitution of such places, shipps, and goods, as were taken from the French in Canida, particularly the Fort of Quebec, his Majestie doth continue his former resolution, declared to the Ambassador by a Memoriall given him in Latin, that the s^d fort and habitason of Quebec, taken by Captayne Kirke, the 9th of July, shall be restored in the same estate as it was taken, without demolishing the fortification or buildings, or carrying away arms, munitions, merchandizes, or utensils, which were there taken; and that if any be taken away, they

shall be either restored in specie, or in value,
according to the proportion, as doth or upon
further examination upon oath, shall appeare
to have been found in the place. In like
manner, such skinnes as were taken and
brought away, as prize or booty, out of the
s^d fort, shall be restored, as doth or shall
appear, upon good account made upon oath,
to have been taken and brought away from
thence.   This His Majestie still resolves to
performe accordinge to His former declaracon,
and doth not affirm that he can further be
prest in this point, by reason of the late
treatye.

2. Touchinge the above, complaynd of
against the English Merchants, for concealing
and imbesilling the skins brought from
Canada, order is given by the Lords of the
Councell, and a Clerke of the Councell, ex-
pressley employed, for a particular search to
be made, and inventory taken of such skinnes
as remayne, and what is defective—to be
supplied by the marchants to the end, all be
performed according to former promise.

3. Concerning such merchandize as Porter de Tasse, and other merchants of Calais, lay clayme unto, as being taken in a ship of Hamburgh, the Lords of the Councell have, according as is required, taken the knowledge of their cause into their hands, with all the documents that belong thereunto, with purpose to have restitution made, as it may appear these goodes do properly belong to the French.

4 and 5. Touching one ship in particular, of S. Johan de Leez, taken by Sir William Alexander, since brought into Plimouth, and three other shippes, the Amity, the Peter, and the Michael of Calais, taken by others, and carryed into Scotland, His Majesty had taken particular order for their restitution."

APPENDIX D.

An Extract of yᵉ Patent granted to Sir William Alexander, concerning Canada.

In yᵉ Commission granted to Sir William Alexander the younger, and others (whereof the Preface alleageth of yᵉ Discovery made by them of a beneficiall Trade for Divers Commoditys, to be had in yᵉ Gulf and River of Canada, and parts adjacent, and His Majestie's resolution thereupon to incorporate them for yᵉ sole trading in those parts, upon a further discovery to be made by them.

The said Sir William Alexander, &c., are assigned as Commissioners for the making of a Voyage into the sᵈ Gulfe and River, and parts adjacent, for yᵉ sole Trade, &c., with power to settle a Plantation within all parts of yᵉ said Gulfe and River, above those parts

which are over against Kebeck, on the S.
side, or above twelve leagues below Tadousach,
on the N. side. Prohibiting all others to
make any voyage into ye s^d Gulfe or River,
or any the parts adjacent to any the pur-
poses aforesaid, upon payne of Confiscation
of their Goods and Shipping so employed,
which ye Commis^{ners} are authorized to seize
unto their own use.

Power given them to make Prize of all
French or Spanish ships and goods at sea
or land, &c., and to displant the French.

Power of Government amongst themselves.

Covenant of further Letters Patent of In-
corporation, or otherwise, for settling the
Trade and Plantation.

Saving of all former Letters Patent.

APPENDIX E..

To all and singuler, as well Nobles and Gentils
as others, to whome these presents shall come
to be seene, read, and heard. I, Richard St.
George, Knighte, Clarencieux Kinge-at-Armes
of y° east, west, and south parts of England
to the river of the Trent, sendeth due com-
mendacons in our Lord God Everlastinge,
forasmuch as ancientlie from the beginninge
the valiant and vertuous actes of worthie persons have been commended to y° world by
sundry monuments and remembrances of theire
chiefest and most good deserts, among which
have been the beareing of signes in shieldes,
called Armes, being evident demonstrations
and tokens of prowesse and valour, diverslie
distributed accordinge to the qualities and
deserts of the persons meritinge the same,

which order as it was prudently devised in the beginninge to stirre and kindle the hearts of men to the imitation of virtue and noblenesse, even soe hath the same been and yet is continuallie observed, to the intent that such as have done commendable service to their Prince or countrie, either in warre or peace, may receive due honor in their lives, and also desire to continue the same successivelie to their posteritie for evermore. Amongst which number Captain David Kirke, eldest sonne and heire of Jervas Kirke, of London, merchant, and late of Deepe, in France, sonne of Thurstan Kirke, of Greenhill, in y⁰ parish of Norton, in y⁰ county of Derby, third sonne of Arnold Kirke, of Whitehough, als Whitehall, which said familie and surname have borne for their coat armour these Armes depicted in the margen, (that is to say) per fesse *or* and *gules* a lozenge counterchanged; but I, the said Clarencieux, being requested by the said Captaine Kirke to give him some addicon of honor of his said armes, and a crest correspondent to the same. Whereuppon I, beinge crediblie informed of the honourable and worthie enterprizes and imployments of the said Captain David Kirke and his brothers, both by sea and land, and that of late being Admirall and Chiefe Commander in the same fleete mett and encountered with the French Navie under the command of Monsieur de Rockmond, Admirall thereof, whom hee and his brothers vanquished and overcame, and brought the said Monsieur de Rockmond prizoner unto England; and y° next yeare followinge the said Captain David Kirke goeinge with His Majesties Commission under the Greate Seale with a fleet of nyne saile for the surprizinge and takinge of the countrie of Canada, in the continent and maineland of America, which was there planted with the French, in which expedition hee and his brothers soe worthilie, and with soe great valour demeaned themselves, that they surprized the French that had there fortifyed themselves, wonne their forte, and took Monsieur Champlaine, their Governor and Chiefe Commander, prisoner, and brought him captive into England. In consideracon whereof, I, the said Kinge of Armes, by power and authoritie under the Greate Seale of England unto my office attributed and annexed, doe by these presents not only ratifie and confirme the said auncient coate, but allso give and graunt to the said Captaine David Kirke, Lewis Kirke, now Captaine and Governor of the sayd fort for his Matie in Canada, Thomas Kirke, Captaine and Vice-Admirall of the said fleete, John and James Kirke, his brothers, the coat armour of Monsieur Rockmond, Admirall of the sayd French Fleete, (that is to say) azure a lion rampant, *or*, supportinge this instrument, *argent*, as it is here portraied, to beare in a canton, as an augmentason or addition of honor, but the lyon to be couchant and collered with a chaine, *argent*, as enthralled and prostrating himselfe to the mercy of the vanquisher. And for his creast on a helmet and wreath of his colours an arme armed proper purpled *or*, holdeinge a curtelas *argent*, hilted *or*, mantled *gules* doubled *argent*, as more plainly appeareth depicted in the margin, all which saide armes and creast with the appurtenances, I, Clarencieux Kinge of Armes, do by these presents allowe, ratifie, and confirm unto the said Captaine Kirke and his brothers, and the yssues of their bodies lawfullie begotten, with due differences. And hee and they the same to use, beare, and shewe forth in a shield, coat armour, or otherwise, aceordinge to y* auncient Lawe of Armes, at his or their libertie and pleasure for evermore. In witnesse whereof, I, the said Kinge of Armes, have hereunto set my hand and seale of office. Dated at London, this First day of December, in the seventh yeare of our Soveraigne Lord Kinge Charles, and in the yeare of our Lord God, 1631.

RICHARD St. GEORGE,
CLARENCIEUX KING OF ARMES.

APPENDIX F.

My most honoured Lords,

Your gracious letters of the 4th of March last, I have received, and by them do perceive that many complaynts by the West Country owners and fishermen, have been made against me to His Majestie and your honours. I most humbly acknowledge myselfe bounde to His Most Gracious Matie and your Lordships, for the good opinion you have of me, and for the reference of them to a further hearinge, either to my condemnation or satisfaction, my innocence being proved. As soon as I received your Lordships' letters, I sent warrants to all Planters and Fishermen, to see all clauses in the 9th of His Majestie's Reigne kept and observed, as also on my part I have done since my commin heither, and will still keepe and observe them, together with every particular contayned in His Maj^{tie's} gracious patent, granted to the Right Honble Ld James Marquess Hambleton, Philipe, Earle of Pemb. and Mont., Henry, Earl of Holland, and myselfe.

I beseech your L^{du} to believe, as I protest before God, all that they have alledged ag^t me is most false; and if, when I am face to face before them and your L^{ships,} any man breathinge can testify one of these complaynts to be true, I will lay downe my heade at your feete, and ever after will be counted unworthy of the service of my gracious Prince and my Lords. I am to give your L^{p's} letters to me for the maintaining of His Ma^{tie's} lawes in the 9th of His Raigne. Many of the fishermen themselves, upon what grounds I know not, have this yeare divine their stages and cooke-roomes in so much, that ye most sevill and wisest men amongst

· them did themselves complaine to me of these outrages, all which passages, and many more whereof, I have good proofes, I hope, to make His Matie and your L^ps acquainted with, and cleare myselfe of all those causless clamours against me; ffor I confesse, he that would interrupt the ffishinge of Newfoundland, which is one of the most considerable Business ffor the Kingdoms of His Matie, and benefit of His subjects and navigation, is worthy the name of a traitour, the least thought and imagination whereof I do abhorre. Soe hoping that His Most Excellent Matie and your Lo^ps will still have that good opinion of me, as I perceive by your gracious letters you have, I shall desire to live no longer then I performe in all duty and sincerity his Matie's service, and ever rest

Your Lo^ps most humble servant,
to His uttmost power,
DAVID KIRKE.

ffereland,

12th of September, 1640.

To the Right Hon^{bles} the L^{ds} of
His Ma^{tie's} most Honble Privee
Counsell put these.

Endorsed,

Septembis, 1640.　Sir David
Kirke.　Newfoundland fishermen.　12 Sep., 1640.

APPENDIX G.

To the King's most excellent Majesty.

The humble petition of Sr Lewys Kirke, John Kirke, and Francis Berkeley, Esquires, sheweth—

That whereas your Majesty's Petitioners have an interest in the Countries of Nova Scotia and Canada, in America, upon the accompt of threescore thousand pounds sterling, dew to your petitioners, upon Articles of Agreement between the French and them, at the surrender of the Fort of Quebec, in the year 1632, according to your Majesty's Father's command of blessed memory.

Your Petitioners humbly pray that the said Countries may not be put into the hands of any other, till your petitioners' grievances are heard, and the annexed reasons be considered of by your Majesty, and those of your Majesty's Privy Counsell shall be appointed to consider thereof, and the rather because noe results have been made by those of the committee of foraigne plantations, to whom your concernments were referred.

ENDORSEMENT.

Whitehall, December 11, 1660.

His Majesty is graciously pleased to referr this Peticon to the Right Honorable the Earl of Lindsey, Lord Great Chamberlain; the Lord Viscount Valentia, Sir Frederick Cornwallis, Treasurer of His Maties Household; Sir Charles Berkeley, Comptroller; Sir George Carter, Vice-Chamberlain; Sir Edward Nicholas and Sir William Morris, Principal Secretaries of State; and Sir Anthony Ashley Cooper, or any four of them, to call Mr. Thomas Elliot and the Peticoners before them, and having heard and examined the business, to make report thereof to His Majestie.

WILLIAM MORIER.

The petition of Francis Kirke, John Kirke,

and Francis Berkeley : Having an interest in
Nova Scotia and Canada upon y⁰ accompt of
60,000 lbs. sterling, due to them upon Articles
of Agreement between y⁰ French and them,
pray yᵗ those country's may not be put into
the hands of any other untill y⁰ Petitioners'
grievances are heard by His Matie, or such
of the Council whom His Matie shall appoint
to hear the said and the reasons annexed.

ENDORSED.

Mr. Elliot and Sir Lewis Kirke to be heard
by counsel.

BEMROSE AND SONS, PRINTERS, LONDON AND DERBY.

Trieste

Trieste Publishing has a massive catalogue of classic book titles. Our aim is to provide readers with the highest quality reproductions of fiction and non-fiction literature that has stood the test of time. The many thousands of books in our collection have been sourced from libraries and private collections around the world.

The titles that Trieste Publishing has chosen to be part of the collection have been scanned to simulate the original. Our readers see the books the same way that their first readers did decades or a hundred or more years ago. Books from that period are often spoiled by imperfections that did not exist in the original. Imperfections could be in the form of blurred text, photographs, or missing pages. It is highly unlikely that this would occur with one of our books. Our extensive quality control ensures that the readers of Trieste Publishing's books will be delighted with their purchase. Our staff has thoroughly reviewed every page of all the books in the collection, repairing, or if necessary, rejecting titles that are not of the highest quality. This process ensures that the reader of one of Trieste Publishing's titles receives a volume that faithfully reproduces the original, and to the maximum degree possible, gives them the experience of owning the original work.

We pride ourselves on not only creating a pathway to an extensive reservoir of books of the finest quality, but also providing value to every one of our readers. Generally, Trieste books are purchased singly - on demand, however they may also be purchased in bulk. Readers interested in bulk purchases are invited to contact us directly to enquire about our tailored bulk rates. Email: customerservice@triestepublishing.com

You May Also Like

ISBN: 9780649663057
Paperback: 188 pages
Dimensions: 6.14 x 0.40 x 9.21 inches
Language: eng

On Spermatorrhœa: Its Pathology, Results, and Complications

J. L. Milton

ISBN: 9780649691807
Paperback: 244 pages
Dimensions: 6.14 x 0.51 x 9.21 inches
Language: eng

Geological Survey of Missouri: A Preliminary Report on the Coal Deposits of Missouri from Field Work Prosecuted During the Years 1890 and 1891

Arthur Winslow

www.triestepublishing.com

You May Also Like

ISBN: 9780649057054
Paperback: 140 pages
Dimensions: 6.14 x 0.30 x 9.21 inches
Language: eng

The University of Minnesota. The Calendar for the Year 1883-84

University Minneapolis

ISBN: 9780649066155
Paperback: 144 pages
Dimensions: 6.14 x 0.31 x 9.21 inches
Language: eng

Heath's Modern Language Series. Atala

François-René de Chateaubriand & Oscar Kuhns

You May Also Like

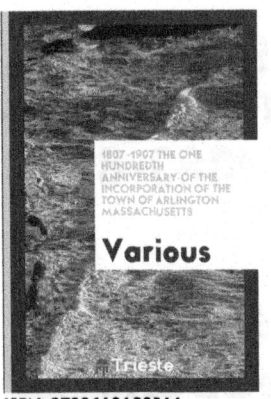

ISBN: 9780649420544
Paperback: 108 pages
Dimensions: 6.14 x 0.22 x 9.21 inches
Language: eng

1807-1907 The One Hundredth Anniversary of the incorporation of the Town of Arlington Massachusetts

Various

ISBN: 9780649194292
Paperback: 44 pages
Dimensions: 6.14 x 0.09 x 9.21 inches
Language: eng

Biennial report of the Board of State Harbor Commissioners, for the two fiscal years commencing July 1, 1890, and ending June 30, 1892

Various

www.triestepublishing.com

You May Also Like

Biennial report of the Board of State Harbor Commissioners for the two fisca years. Commeneing July 1, 1884, and Ending June 30, 1886

Various

ISBN: 9780649199693
Paperback: 48 pages
Dimensions: 6.14 x 0.10 x 9.21 inches
Language: eng

Biennial report of the Board of state commissioners, for the two fiscal years, commencing July 1, 1890, and ending June 30, 1892

Various

ISBN: 9780649196395
Paperback: 44 pages
Dimensions: 6.14 x 0.09 x 9.21 inches
Language: eng

Find more of our titles on our website. We have a selection of thousands of titles that will interest you. Please visit

www.triestepublishing.com

Lightning Source UK Ltd.
Milton Keynes UK
UKOW01f1852161017
311093UK00005B/155/P

9 780649 583454